"Positing that the ancient beginni
ple rather than with the trader, an
not just the secular use of money,
orful mosaic of personal, historica
perspectives regarding this important dimension of life. In communities of faith that seek to live a world-formative rather than a
world-de   mportant
but often   ry church
small gro

es Ringma
nt Wisdom

"Through the heart is the deepest, truest way that we learn about
things that matter most—and that is the great gift of this new book
by Clive Lim and Paul Stevens, who together draw on the years of
their lives to allow us to think more carefully and critically, and
therefore more Christianly, about the meaning of money. From its
first pages we are graced with their wisdom and experience born of
rare biblical and theological insight integrally connected to cultural
and historical perspectives, all twined together with decades of life
in the world of work. In *Money Matters*, these master teachers ad-
dress the most challenging questions and the most difficult issues,
ones that serious people the world over wrestle with about money,
and why it matters so much."

— Steven Garber
author of *The Seamless Life:
A Tapestry of Love and Learning, Worship and Work*

"Thinking *Christianly* about money is one of the more important,
but also one of the more difficult challenges facing the followers
of Christ today, in the East as well as in the West. By grounding
their consideration of money in their own very different personal
narratives—East and West—Lim and Stevens treat their readers

with wisdom as well as any number of important insights into the ubiquitous role that money plays in our lives today."

— **Craig Gay**
author of *Modern Technology and the Human Future:*
A Christian Appraisal

"*Money Matters* is a must read for those who are concerned with handling earthly wealth with the Kingdom of God in mind. By integrating biblical and theological foundations, it reminds us of the spiritual roots of money and our stewardship role in God's plan, sparking our creativity to truly honor God with the use of money."

— **William Chen**
chairman, Crown Financial Ministries, Hong Kong

"Paul and Clive, in their excellent treatise on money, have helped uncover fresh depths of biblical understanding on this age-old yet poorly understood subject. Their erudite scholarship makes for a solidly biblical exegesis on money. As the book reminds us, money is the barometer of the soul. Yet the pulpit pays scant attention to money other than the obvious subject of tithes and offerings. It is no wonder that many believers succumb to several fallacies: in particular, a dualism that dichotomizes the secular and the sacred. Paul and Clive convincingly demolish this divide that has distorted the Christian worldview. They also challenge the widely held notion that views money as neutral. The book is a much-needed resource to help believers capture a holistic understanding of money and dispels several fallacies on this important subject."

— **Georgie Lee**
national president, Gatekeepers Singapore

"Like Clive, I grew up poor in Singapore, and like Paul, I lived in North America, for a time, and witnessed its affluence. What a treat to have both authors bringing together East and West with such contrasting worldviews to bear on such a controversial issue as money. Their experiences and insights, disciplined by a clear biblical perspective, give us valuable scrutiny of the cracks in dualism, capitalism, and, most of all, the prosperity gospel. While we cannot serve God and money, this book will open our minds and hearts to serve God with money."

— **David W. F. Wong**
leadership mentor, Finishing Well Ministries

"Few people in the faith, work, and economics movement have been as influential as R. Paul Stevens. His books on the intersections of religious belief and economic activity are legendary, and they continue to inspire and challenge generations of Christians in the marketplace. Now, with coauthor Clive Lim, Stevens has ventured into new territory with *Money Matters*, a unique and fascinating look at the fruits of our labor. Beginning with their own life stories, the authors delve deeply into cultural and biblical narratives about wealth, toppling the idols of both unbridled capitalism and the 'health and wealth gospel' along the way. The fundamental thrust of the book may be their unabashed claim that money isn't morally neutral and that God cares deeply about our relationship with it. Either way, for those wishing to put mammon in its proper place and deploy it for Kingdom purposes, this book is required reading and will no doubt become another classic in the faith, work, and economics space."

— **Kenneth J. Barnes**
author of *Redeeming Capitalism*

"Paul Stevens and Clive Lim seek to engage readers in personal contemplation that enables them to view money 'in its proper place and to behave with consistency in relation to the handling of money.' They have achieved their purpose quite nicely. Every serious Christian should have a personal view of money, especially in the handling of it. Blending their differing experience and expertise (in terms of age, training, aptitude, upbringing, ethnicity, etc.), the authors are comfortable with each other, complementing each other as they canvass related issues and viewpoints from historical, contemporary, social, and theological angles. The topics are well-chosen and relevant. And the book is very readable; one can finish it either in a three-to-four-hour sitting or over several days, taking the time to study the issues raised more contemplatively, taking in the endnotes. Hence, there is something in this book for everyone!"

— Ho Peng Kee
former senior minister of state in Singapore

"*Money Matters* is the most relevant and expansive discussion on money. Period. It is personal and deep, as Stevens and Lim share stories of decades of business experience with deep theological reflection. They show how our relationship with money permeates our identity, determines how we run our businesses and organizations, and reflects what we truly value. For a topic that is often confusing and overlooked, *Money Matters* offers clarity, hope, and a challenge to live our lives intentionally for the Kingdom in a way that is life changing and impactful. Who could imagine a book about money could be so inspiring?"

— Dave Hataj
author of *Good Work: How Blue Collar Business Can Change Lives, Communities, and the World*

Money Matters

Faith, Life, and Wealth

R. Paul Stevens
Clive Lim

WILLIAM B. EERDMANS PUBLISHING COMPANY
GRAND RAPIDS, MICHIGAN

Wm. B. Eerdmans Publishing Co.
4035 Park East Court SE, Grand Rapids, Michigan 49546
www.eerdmans.com

27 26 25 24 23 22 21   1 2 3 4 5 6 7

ISBN 978-0-8028-7751-2

Library of Congress Cataloging-in-Publication Data

Names: Stevens, R. Paul, 1937– author. | Lim, Clive C. H., 1958– author.
Title: Money matters : faith, life, and wealth / R. Paul Stevens, Clive Lim.
Description: Grand Rapids, Michigan : William B. Eerdmans Publishing
  Company, 2021. | Includes bibliographical references and index. | Sum-
  mary: "A guide to navigating money and matters of economics from a
  biblically informed, faith-driven perspective"—Provided by publisher.
Identifiers: LCCN 2020028359 | ISBN 9780802877512 (paperback)
Subjects: LCSH: Wealth—Religious aspects—Christianity. | Money—Reli-
  gious aspects—Christianity.
Classification: LCC BR115.W4 S74 2021 | DDC 241/.68—dc23
LC record available at https://lccn.loc.gov/2020028359

To Michelle (Clive's wife) and Gail (Paul's wife),
blessed companions for whom we thank God, who have
accompanied us on our life journeys, especially as they relate to
money, spirituality, and everyday practice

Contents

Introduction

*The gods we worship write their names on our faces, be
sure of that. . . . We may think that our tribute is paid
in secret in the dark recesses of the heart—but it will
out. That which dominates our imagination and our
thoughts will determine our life and character. Therefore it behooves us to be careful what we are worshipping, for what we are worshipping, we are becoming.*

Gates of Prayer,
a Reform Jewish prayer book[1]

Why is money so central, so ubiquitous, so engaging, and so powerful that people say "money talks"? That is what we must find
out, and specifically we must discover how we are to use money
wisely and even redemptively. But why do two authors take on
this assignment?

This is an East-West book. Clive Lim comes from Singapore,
works as a business entrepreneur, and serves as a part-time theological educator. Paul Stevens, who is from Vancouver, Canada, has
pastored churches, been a carpenter, run a business, and more recently has been a professor of marketplace theology. We start the
book with our own stories: Clive growing up without money; Paul
growing up with money. We do this because we all are on journeys

with respect to money, and everyone's journey is influenced by family, culture of origin, and, as we shall see, faith or lack of faith.

In the West, where Paul lives, we can talk about sex freely. Sometimes we can talk a little about our relationship with God, but money is the last silent sanctuary. The fig leaf has slipped over the wallet. In the East, where Clive lives, money is the easiest thing to talk about. You come back from a vacation: "How much did you spend?" You go to someone's apartment or home: "Very nice. What did you pay for it?" You get a new job: "How much are you making?" But the fig leaf is firmly secured over the genitals in the East. So we will explore cultural differences, because we all live today in a global culture and a global economy.

It hardly needs confirmation that money is an important part of everyday life for individuals as well as a crucial dimension of the productivity of the whole society. Jesus must have understood this, because he talked more about money than prayer and heaven. And the reason is clear. Money grabs the heart. It is not neutral. It is a power. It can be a radioactive issue. We want to have money, but money wants to have us. And at the same time, money is a barometer of the soul. It tells what we value, what we consider for our security, and what we worship. Yes, money is a problem, but it is also a blessing and even a sacrament. To get at this we want to tell our own stories.

The Book in Brief

So after we have shared some of our own money stories in the first two chapters, we plunge into the religious history of money in chapter three—how it has been associated with temples and sacred things from the beginning. But then in chapter four, we explore a shrewd saying of Jesus to examine a critical dimension that comes out of the history of money: whether we can have a single vision, a unitary consciousness about the handling of money. Referring to a statement by Jesus that we will explore further, we ask, is it possible to give to Caesar (that is, to our earthly financial obligations) and give to God *at the same time*? Not surprisingly, after that, we step back to look at the larger money picture, the whole monetary system, and ask how we can deal with capitalism. Chapter five is a primer on the system that dominates the world and has, for many, become a form of religion.

Refocusing again on the personal in chapter six, we explore an outrageous parable of Jesus in which he tells us to use money to make friends who will last forever and who will welcome us into heaven. Obviously, we cannot buy friendship, but what can Jesus possibly mean? Then, once again, in chapter seven, we take another wide-angle view of money as we consider social values, how our handling of money reflects gender differences, Eastern and Western cultural values, and how we tend to earmark money by means of its sources, good and bad, sacred or profane. This chapter ends with a short note on the emerging cryptocurrency. But all these considerations raise the question of stewardship in chapter eight, as stewardship is that overarching concept of being trusted with something for the benefit of others. So we will research the implications of the truth that God is the owner of everything, including our money, and how we should then live with money. But chapter eight ends with some reflections on the Christian church and its stewardship, including our financial support of Christian workers.

This leads us into chapter nine where we evaluate a very significant money movement in the global Christian church: the health and wealth gospel. Here we reflect on whether our faith can make us wealthy in this life. But in the last chapter, ten, we suggest rather teasingly how we might become wealthy in the next life through investment in heaven. And just how can we do this? That is the journey we are taking in the book.

xiv   INTRODUCTION

What Can You Expect?

You will gain a clear understanding of what money means, what money does, and what money cannot do. You will know where money has come from. You will see that our relationship with money is not external to our spirituality but is deeply personal and revelatory. Money reveals the heart, grabs people, and makes almost godlike claims on the heart, as suggested by our use of the common phrase "the almighty dollar." You will understand how the big economic system operates, how it needs mending, and yet how it has brought relief from poverty to millions, all the while, unfortunately, widening the gap between rich and poor. And you will discover that Scripture provides an extraordinary perspective on money and what we should do with it. But the perspective of Scripture raises a problem. Earlier we said that money was a blessing, a sacrament, and a problem. Here is why.

The Ambiguity of Scripture on Money

The Old Testament, or Hebrew Bible, in particular, presents wealth mainly as a blessing. Scripture promises the Israelites material blessing as a reward for obedience. "If you fully obey the LORD your God and carefully follow all his commands. . . . The LORD will open the heavens, the storehouse of his bounty . . . to bless all the work of your hands" (Deut. 28:1, 12). Abraham, Isaac, and Jacob, along with King Solomon and Job, were blessed with wealth. But these Old Testament "saints" were people who depended on God, not on their wealth, in contrast to those who praised the Lord because they were rich (Zech. 11:5). Money, and lots of it, is a kind of sacrament bringing blessing and help, "a gift of God," as the professor says (Eccles. 5:19). But that same professor (*ekklesiastēs* means a leader of a community) reflects on his life with and without God and crafts two strange and seemingly oxymoronic sentences: "Money is the

answer for everything" (Eccles. 10:19) and "Whoever loves money
never has enough" (5:10). Insightfully, Jacob Needleman in *Money
and the Meaning of Life* remarks, "Money can buy almost anything
we want—the problem being that we tend to want only the things
that money can buy."[2]

So alongside the blessing of wealth, the Old Testament affirms
that the pursuit of wealth for its own sake is a vain, destructive thing
leading to self-destructive autonomy (Prov. 30:8–9).[3] Wealth will not
satisfy (Eccles. 5:10). So when we come to the health and wealth gospel in the second-to-last chapter of the book, we will show how this
movement misinterprets God's deepest concerns for us in claiming
that God's promises to Israel apply immediately and completely
to Christians today. According to the Old Testament, money is a
blessing, a sacrament, and a problem. Craig L. Blomberg, a biblical
theologian, summarizes the two testaments this way: "Wealth as a
sign of God's blessing and as a reward for one's labor, then, are the
two major strands of Old Testament teaching that for the most part
do *not* carry over into the New Testament."[4] He continues, aptly,
"The Covenant model that assumes that material reward for piety
never reappears in Jesus' teaching, and is explicitly contradicted
throughout."[5] So in the New Testament the "wealth as a problem"
dimension gets deeper treatment.

The apostle Paul warns that "Those who want to get rich fall into
temptation and a trap and into many foolish and harmful desires
that plunge people into ruin and destruction. For the love of money
is a root of all kinds of evil" (1 Tim. 6:9–10). Jesus himself talked a lot
about money and said that our pursuit of earthly wealth affects the
heart: "Where your treasure is, there your heart will be also" (Matt.
6:21). Most challenging is how Jesus calls some people to sell all they
have and give to the poor in order to have treasure in heaven (see
Matt. 19:21). We will explore these challenging words, but we will
do so from the major perspective we bring to the study of money
yesterday, today, and forever.

The Kingdom Perspective

The transformative perspective of Jesus on all of life's issues, including money, is the present and future irruption of the kingdom of God.[6] This coming of God's kingdom is Jesus's master thought. He speaks of it over a hundred times in the four Gospels. It radically affected how he viewed money, both the pursuit of it and the investment of it. The gospel he proclaimed was not the gospel of soul-salvation but the good news that the kingdom of God had come and was coming fully at the end of history. The kingdom is God's intervening in the world, bringing human flourishing and transformation in the deepest sense. Blomberg succinctly summarizes the core of Jesus's ministry:

> God's dynamic reign has broken into human history through [Jesus's] person and ministry in a new and decisive way and . . . God intends to create a new community of his people who model, at least in part in the present, what God intends for all humanity and what he will one day perfectly create in a new age.[7]

So one way of speaking of the kingdom of God is this: *God's new world coming* (both now and ultimately later, both here and coming). It starts with the soul but encompasses everything, including our use of money.

The kingdom of God is an integrating theme of the entire Bible, though the term "kingdom" is not always used. From the beginning God intended to exercise his sovereignty through his entire creation. In the creation story God commissioned a God-imaging creature (humankind) to flesh out that purpose in all of life and all of creation. Old Testament professor Bruce Waltke puts it this way: "I argue that *adam* (i.e. humankind) is created to establish God's kingdom."[8] Sin disrupted the program but grace has largely restored God's intention of bringing transformation to all people and all creation.

So we must ask some questions.

How can we use money in a kingdom way in the presence of an anti-kingdom context? Is money itself something created by God and for God but which has become corrupted and tainted, taking on a life of its own? Can it be redeemed? How do we handle money in a kingdom way (which is to ask the stewardship question)? Does our use of money reflect the values of the kingdom of God? Just how can we invest money in the kingdom of God? And how can we invest in the fulfilled kingdom in the new heaven and new earth?

Yes, this book is written by two followers of Jesus. But you will find, we trust, that we are dealing with universals, even with concepts that can be found in many faiths. And we invite you not only to hear about our journey but also to review your own journey and travel with us in our experience of money. Money, we will see, is not simply a medium of exchange—and not a simple medium at all! Now, for our stories.

1

Growing Up without Money—Clive's Story

To study money is to study a very large part of what we are.

Jacob Needleman[1]

I was trying to sleep, but the urgency of my parents' voices kept me alert. In the dark of the bedroom, my three other siblings were breathing deeply and evenly, sound asleep. I thought, I must stay awake. My parents' voices were desperate. Something must be wrong. As I listened intently, I realized they were talking about money—once again—about paying some outstanding bills. My parents kept their money struggles from us, but their anxiety about the lack of money always seemed to crop up in their conversations.

The night air in our tiny room was heavy with tension. How was a child supposed to help his parents with their financial burdens? My parents never directly shared with us children their struggles with money, difficulties that frequently erupted into quarrels. So as a child I would lie in bed and fantasize about money. I dreamed of buying the candies and chocolates I saw on television advertisements. But most urgently I fantasized that my parents would stop quarrelling and my father would not have to work every day so he could spend more time at home with us. I imagined my pockets were filled with a thick wad of currency. In my fantasy I felt safe and gradually drifted into a quiet sleep.

Growing Up in Singapore—the Family Background

Life in post-colonial Singapore in the early 1960s was hard. Crimes were rife, and labor and racial disputes sometimes erupted into riots during which buildings and possessions were burned. Jobs were scarce, and many who did work were not compensated fairly or their salaries were delayed. And they did not dare dispute with unscrupulous bosses for fear of losing their jobs. My father worked for more than a decade as a clerk in a restaurant and lost all his pension when his employer fled Singapore, leaving a mountain of unpaid debts. Dad was an honest and hardworking man. He worked tirelessly seven days a week. But eventually he was stricken with tuberculosis.

My parents were the children of South China's migrants and grew up during the Second World War's Japanese occupation of Singapore. My father had a few years of schooling and toiled in menial jobs most of his life to provide for the family. Dad never had a stable job long enough to afford a home. Our family rented a poorly built government apartment that was our only home for the first thirty years of my life. There were two bedrooms, but to supplement the family income, my parents rented out one of the rooms. All six of us—my parents, my three siblings, and I—lived and slept in one room until we children were in our teens. In that cramped situation we were always fighting for space and marking out which corners belonged to whom.

We had enough to eat every day but it was all my parents could afford. Money for education and medical treatments was borrowed from reluctant friends and families, who were themselves struggling financially. In spite of our limited resources, my father was a generous person, always sharing with relatives who were in even deeper financial straits. Chinese New Year is a big event for all Chinese families around the world. For us it was a treat to expect new clothes, shoes, and better food. The best meals were prepared for us to eat together as a family. I later realized that this was a financial burden for my parents as they scraped together enough money to buy new clothes and provisions. Many families accumulated debt in order to obtain these gifts, but they did it to ensure that the coming year would be auspicious.

Life was very different for my mother during her childhood. She grew up in a sizable home in Singapore that housed three generations. They were a business family and owned large tracts of land, the equivalent of a small modern-day supermarket, a food manufacturing business, and a farm. As a child, my mother had her own personal maid. But at the age of nine, her whole life radically changed. As the Japanese Imperial soldiers marched into Singapore in early 1942, the local residents reacted in fear and started rioting. The supermarket was raided, all the provisions and stocks were looted, and the premises were wrecked. The food business and the land were confiscated by the occupying Japanese forces. A family business that was built over two generations disappeared, never to be resurrected. Within weeks of the Japanese occupation, the family's businesses were gone and a new life of hardship began for my mother's family.

My maternal grandfather and grandmother were versatile and adjusted to a new way of life as farmers. Eventually, however, even the family home and farm were repossessed by the new independent government, and my grandparents were reduced to subsistence farming on a small plot of land beside a cemetery. As young children, my siblings and I would play in that cemetery, using the tombstones as cover for our games of hide and seek. When I became a teenager, I earned pocket money during the weekends by helping my grandfather collect leftover food from the surrounding residences and bringing it to the farm. Over a big fire and huge wok, the leftovers were recooked as food for the pigs and chickens that my maternal grandparents were raising. That pattern of hardship continued in my father's life.

Life for my dad was always hard. As a child, he lost his father, and both his sisters died from heart disease in their early adult lives. My paternal grandparents were migrants from South China and came to Singapore as farmers to operate a small plot of ground as a vegetable farm. Dad left school after my grandfather died from a tropical illness, and Dad started working when he was barely a teenager. Though he had a few years of schooling, for several decades my father fondly kept a box of books he planned to read. But as a young man he was tragically hit by a military truck and lost part of his hearing. He never fully regained his health. He was diligent and eager to work every day but frequently found himself without work when the businesses he worked for had their mortgages foreclosed or voluntarily shut down. Life was easier when we children started working, but eventually my father succumbed to illness after turning seventy years old.

Study Hard and Earn Lots of Money

"Without money you are nothing." My parents frequently drilled this into me as a child. My financially stricken parents wanted a better life for me. The only way out of their endless toil, they thought, was to gain the ability to earn more money. Their advice was simple: you need to study hard to earn lots of money. Unfortunately, education among the millions of struggling Chinese diaspora was never a quest for knowledge for the betterment of oneself but a means of social elevation and survival. For thousands of years, Chinese society has been highly hierarchical and stratified. The only means of social elevation was by way of scholastic examinations. Top scholars were rewarded with juicy civil service jobs. This is still the practice in contemporary Singapore, where students are selected during high school to be placed in a scholastic program that will lead to plum civil service jobs.

So you can see how my sense of identity and well-being is enmeshed with money. For my family, money is indeed the answer to everything! Money is the hope of a better life. So in the eyes of our family and culture, being a good man equals being a good provider. An honest husband and father who struggles to provide for his family is somehow a lesser person than a rich husband and father who provides abundantly, even though he may have multiple wives. Money gives a feeling of omnipotence and the person who has great earning ability has tremendous influence over family members and relatives and is usually forgiven for many sins.

During the first thirty years of my life, all my decisions aimed at making money. I chose my studies based on the potential remuneration of various jobs. I looked for work by comparing monetary compensations. Even though I hated the jobs I had and dreaded going to work every morning, I consoled myself that the monthly pay check was enough compensation for my drudgeries. Looking back, I realize my anxieties about money blinded me to my need to find my calling. So the more I focused on money, the unhappier I became. But in spite of this, I had a goal.

For many years I carried a note, the size of a business card, in my wallet. It read, "I shall become a millionaire by 35 years of age." I faithfully read it several times a day in an attempt to remind myself of my life goal and to visualize the path I would take to arrive at my goal. I grew up in scarcity and was determined not to struggle for the rest of my life. So I had a plan.

I started my working life loaded with debt. I borrowed money to finish my business education and then took a loan to throw a wedding dinner and to give a dowry for my bride. Money was very tight. I budgeted my daily expenses and drank plain water with my meals instead of spending money for additional beverages. Ironically, even today I am back to drinking plain water with my meals—for health reasons. When my wife and I moved into our new home, it was sparsely furnished with secondhand furniture, and it took several years before we were able to complete furnishing the apartment. My wife mended our torn sofa so many times, one stitching on top of the other, that once a guest took notice and asked in deep concern how we were doing financially. I needed a car for my work and bought a small, secondhand truck. That became the talk of my colleagues, who were driving luxurious cars. I was relentless in my budgeting and determined to become debt-free.

Money and a Bumpy Spiritual Journey

A gradual and deep shift in my relationship with money took place during my thirties and continues to this day. When I was thirty, some of my colleagues invited me to their church. The one time I had previously been to church was during Christmas when I was a student. We were offered candies and invited to sing with the congregation. But church was "out of bounds" in my family, as my father feared that conversion to Christianity would lead us to abandon our Chinese culture and family. Even before I started going to church, I was always more religious than my siblings and frequently accompanied my mother to Taoist and Buddhist temples. I was a sickly child and frequently had to be in bed several weeks at a time, delirious with fever. My mother was anxious that I might have inadvertently offended the gods and so had brought bad fortune and ill health on myself. My family was not very religious, but my parents believed that it was better to appease these gods and please them than to offend them. In my young mind, these gods seemed rather frivolous, petty, and vindictive, much like human beings. I did not want to have anything to do with them. But in the church it was different.

In the beginning, I was curious about the how the church operated, particularly the function of the pastor. Unlike in the temples I visited as a child, where the priests were poorly educated and not trained, in the churches, Christian pastors were university graduates usually with postgraduate degrees in theology. The Singapore economy in the 1980s was developing briskly, the demand for bankers, lawyers, doctors, and accountants was high, and these jobs were handsomely remunerated. Why would someone, I reflected, with such education choose not to make a good living as a professional and so fulfill the responsibilities to provide for his or her family? But as I continued to visit the church and engaged the pastors with my questions, I became increasingly fascinated with Christianity.

I found church surprising. Everyone seemed friendly and welcoming without any obvious motivation apart from genuine hospitality. I was fascinated by the learned and carefully crafted preaching. After I became a Christian, I read about St. Augustine's conversion and his first impression of Ambrose, the bishop of Milan: "My pleasure was in the charm of his language. It was more learned than that of Faustus, but less witty and entertaining. . . ."[2] The demeanor of the pastor intrigued me. He bore himself with both dignity and humility. He spoke as a well-educated and intelligent person yet with obvious compassion and kindness. I wondered why he was willing to serve as a poorly paid Christian pastor. What was behind such a commitment? I returned every Sunday to listen to the preaching. "Gradually, though I did not realise it, I was drawing closer to God," as Augustine said of himself centuries ago.[3] When we were both thirty, married with a three-month-old infant, my wife and I decided to embrace the Christian faith. I did not discover God. He was looking out for me and waiting for me. "But God demonstrates his own love for us in this: While we were still sinners, Christ died for us" (Rom. 5:8).

A bumpy spiritual journey had begun. Raised in a Confucian family with a conservative and patriarchal father, I was taught to respect and obey my parents, especially my father. Any disagreement with him was rebellion. In our culture, the relationship between father and son preceded all other relationships. Showing respect and obedience to your father is the highest honor a son can show his father. In a Chinese family, filial piety is the highest virtue. This influenced my spiritual journey.

My relationship with God developed in the same direction. I saw God as a "super father," all-powerful, demanding, and deserving of obedience, a virtue that was ingrained in me as a child. I projected my own distant and strained relationship with my father onto my relationship with God. It took me many years to realize that God is not a distant "super father," remote and disapproving. Only when I realized that God is a "compassionate and gracious God, slow to anger, abounding in love and faithfulness" (Exod. 34:6) did I venture into coming near to him and develop a personal relationship with him. Now as an enthusiastic new believer, I wanted to make my faith an integral part of my whole life. There was a problem, however, with my entanglement with money.

I still wanted to be rich. But I always had this nagging feeling that I should be a pastor or missionary, because that is what all Christians seem to aspire to become. I prayed about it and struggled for discernment. I honestly did not feel that I was ready to be a pastor or a missionary. My pastor himself was trained to be a banker but studied to be a pastor after a mission trip. But wisely, my pastor encouraged me to continue to work as a business executive if that was how I discerned God leading me. But he also made it clear that I should, however, set aside time to volunteer in church ministries as a way to serve God and others. So I continued my preoccupation with money.

I put myself into the grind. I traveled incessantly and worked twelve hours a day at my managerial job. I was promoted every year and became the youngest senior manager in a multinational corporation. I was totally preoccupied with my work, driven negatively by fear and positively with the promise of success. Though I wanted to be rich, it began to dawn on me that I was really seeking security. I dreaded the struggles that my parents had to go through to make ends meet. So I put everything on hold: time with my parents, as well as time with my wife and children. I will have time for them, so I thought, once I reach my financial goals. I still remembered the card I carried in my wallet years ago, "I shall become a millionaire by 35 years of age." A couple of years after I became a Christian, I decided to tear up the card but the desire for money remained. By my early thirties I was quickly advancing in my career in an American multinational based in Singapore. I was poised to become a vice president, but I was constantly nagged by a deep desire to start my own business. I was an executive but wanted to become an entrepreneur in order to achieve my financial goals. This is not as easy as it seems, especially when you have a family.

Becoming an Entrepreneur

When I expressed my desires to leave my job, my family and particularly my parents were puzzled and confused. I was advancing in my career far beyond my years and had a tremendous prospect in the new and growing wireless telecommunication industry. Why was I leaving a well paid and stable job to take unnecessary risks? Some of my family considered my behavior irresponsible and naive. My uncle was sent to talk some sense into me by highlighting how difficult it would be to start a business and how inexperienced I was. I understood my parents' anxieties. I had all the opportunities and stability they never had.

It seemed to them that I was throwing away all my blessings. In spite of all this, I left the American multinational and before my thirty-sixth birthday decided to become an entrepreneur. I felt I had waited long enough and had already passed my thirty-five-year age target to become a millionaire.

My new venture expanded quickly and money started flowing. We grew from two employees to two hundred within two years. Now I faced a new problem. In the first part of my life I struggled with scarcity and now, having met my money goal, I had more than I needed. And I learned another ugly truth about money. When we do not have enough we fight one another; we fight even harder when there is too much. The business was doubling in size every year, had expanded into the Asian region, and was poised to grow even further. But success brought a tension I had never expected.

My business partner and I, both Christians, started having disagreements. Our differences escalated. He wanted full control. I resisted. The animosity grew and resentment filled our hearts. I believe Christ was at work during this period of my life even though I failed to see him (see Rom. 8:28). I was working eighty hours a week and enjoying my newfound success thoroughly. I started working before dawn and sprinted through the day in exhilaration, frequently skipping meals. I sighed every evening when the sun set and darkness came. There was still so much to be done! Eventually I would say to the Lord about this period, "Nobody could stop my frantic drive for success and wealth but you, Lord. You stopped me right in the middle of my swelling pride and money-making." I was struck with a mysterious malaise, shivering in the heat of the day, growing weaker and thinner with the weeks. I started coughing blood. I had to slow down.

After several months, my illness was eventually diagnosed, and I was successfully treated and told to rest. I was barely into my late thirties and had never taken an extended break in my life. My illness made me face the possibility of death. I reflected on how short life is on this earth, and lamented on how little time I had spent with the people I love. I acknowledged the Lord's hand in my illness. "The LORD disciplines those he loves, as a father the son he delights in" (Prov. 3:12). After many agonizing months, I peacefully decided to sell my stake to my partners and leave the business I had started. I took a year of sabbatical before my fortieth birthday. But what next?

At forty I was too young to retire. I seriously contemplated God's call for my life and discerned that I should return to business after my sabbatical. This time, when I eventually returned to work, I felt more relaxed and balanced. I avoided staying late in the office and took my holidays assiduously. I had dinner at home every evening with my family when I was not traveling. The flame of my old ambition of wealth was still there, but it had begun to flicker and no longer consumed me. I also learned something about retirement: I don't like it! I will never retire fully from work but will continue to seek meaningful work, paid or voluntary, according to my ability and capacity, as I age.

Your Money or Your Life!

I had met my financial goals and was elated. Unfortunately, that elation lasted only a few weeks. I expected the euphoria when I would reach financial nirvana to be exhilarating, but it was brief and passing. Life goes on. The mundane continues. Whether it is eating, washing, or cleaning, it needs to be done repeatedly. I was disappointed. Wealth promises much but delivers little. Yes, with money life was much easier. I could afford the best food and clothes and pay for domestic help, but it did not make life more meaningful. It was suddenly too easy. But the omnipotence of money continued to be a distraction. I was frequently tempted to use money to solve problems quickly rather than to think deeply about these challenges. Paul was right when he advised the young Timothy, "Command those who are rich in this present world not to be arrogant nor to put their hope in wealth, which is so uncertain, but to put their hope in God, who richly provides us with everything for our enjoyment" (1 Tim. 6:17). I felt short-changed by my money goal. I asked myself whether my life would have taken a different course if I had not been so fixated on money. I wanted a noble cause for my life.

Actually, my newfound wealth gave me some freedom. I had been so preoccupied with achieving my financial goals that I had little time with my family, little time for thinking deeply about my faith. The one-year sabbatical was transformational for my family and for my faith. I developed a new intimacy both with my family and with God. I started experimenting with new businesses, starting an investment firm and a wireless telecommunication distribution company. Both businesses continue to be viable nearly two decades later. So wealth gave me the ability to experiment and develop new experiences and relationships. Having grown up poor and becoming suddenly rich, I recalled, "The wealth of the rich is their fortified city, but poverty is the ruin of the poor" (Prov. 10:15). But there is another side to what the Proverbs say.

My wealth was also a new source of anxiety. I am still preoccupied with money but for a different reason. The scarcity of my childhood instilled discipline and hard work, but now I am worried that our wealth might make my three children indifferent to the poor and to God. I am reminded about this truth in the Bible, the other side of the Proverbs: "Keep falsehood and lies far from me; give me neither poverty nor riches, but give me only my daily bread. Otherwise, I may have too much and disown you and say, 'Who is the LORD?'" (Prov. 30:8–9). To grow up in plenty with every desire pampered is not a good thing. How can one turn to God if life is too easy? How our children deal with money is not just a product of their upbringing but can be a gift from God. I have seen children from wealthy families who are good stewards of money.

My own education about money is not over at this point in my life. I am still tempted by the power of money. For a decade I was buying houses, rebuilding and refurbishing them, renting, living in, and reselling them. It became a new venture after I developed a deep curiosity about building and refurbishing homes. It was hard and anxious work, very different from the financial and telecommunication industries I had spent decades nurturing. One day I suddenly realized the reason for all this. I was accumulating too many properties because my family had never owned a home while I was growing up. I struggled with this verse in the Bible: "Woe to you who add house to house and join field to field till no space is left and you live alone in the land" (Isa. 5:8). My relationship with money exposed my struggles, dreams, and dysfunctions. Through it I was gaining an understanding of myself.

Jacob Needleman, professor of philosophy at San Francisco State University, argues in his book *Money and the Meaning of Life*[4] that our relationship with money is revelatory. "Money enters so deeply into our personality and into our psychophysical organism," he says, "that the personal exploration of money is necessary for the discovery of oneself, the discovery of those hidden parts of human nature that hold prisoner energies that need to be in relationship to our consciousness."[5] Needleman is on a lifelong quest to integrate wisdom and great spiritual learnings with how we can live our contemporary lives effectively. And this takes place in our relationship with money. He laments our lack of honesty with money. "Yet very few of us are unflinchingly honest about our relationship to money. It's like sex was 50 years ago in our culture, a force that operates everywhere, and yet one that very few of us can face squarely and honestly." He argues we are "not to despise [money], and not to be devoured by it, but to take it seriously and study it" in order to understand who we are. [6]

By avoiding the subject of money in our conversations, we move money into our personal and private realms and gradually hide our thoughts on money even from ourselves. We develop a duality, on the one hand, dealing with money in a manner acceptable within the church and, on the other hand, burying our values regarding money in our deepest self, hidden from the public and church view. So how we value and deal with money can even create dissonances within ourselves. In this book we are examining our relationship with money. But we are also discovering something about ourselves. As Jacob Needleman said, "To study money is to study a very large part of what we are."

That is true whether we grew up *without* money, as I did, or *with* money, as Paul did, as he now tells his own story.

2

Growing Up with Money—Paul's Story

Life is lived forward but understood backwards.

Søren Kierkegaard[1]

"It's only money," as my father often said. But I was feeling bad that once again my stupidity had cost my father and mother a lot of money. I was a university student home for the weekend and having borrowed the family car to see my girlfriend in Hamilton, Ontario— now my wife—I returned the car to the driveway. But I failed to put on the parking brake. It rolled slowly backwards down the driveway without a driver! I watched, eyes riveted, as I saw it smash sideways into a telephone pole. The whole side of the car was pushed in. Dad said, "It's only money." Actually my father loved *making* money as a business person but he did not love money. This is an important distinction. But there is more to my education in money than my father's extraordinary attitude.

Clive and I are telling our money stories because our attitude toward money is formed through many influences, not least our family education, our experience growing up, and the influence of our culture. Sometimes the teaching of the church on money, whenever it happens, pales in significance before the overwhelming influence of the media, the culture, and the family in which we grew up. There is precious little church teaching on the subject even though the Bible is chock full of it (except of course the teaching to give one tenth to the church). But we also saw in Clive's story how our experience with money reveals a lot about ourselves. We get to know ourselves partly through our handling of money. What was also evident as Clive told his story was this: our relationship with God is partially shaped by our handling of money. And the reverse is also true: our faith influences our approach to money, especially our view of the kingdom of God. But that is to run ahead of where we are traveling in this book. My story starts with two immigrant parents, one from England and the other from an English colony, Newfoundland, now Canada's most eastern province.

Immigrating to Canada

My father did not have a lot of money in his youth until he became president of a steel fabrication company. Dad grew up in a "just above" poverty situation. He arrived in Canada as a two year old as part of an immigrant group from England. His father was a pastry baker in a Salvation Army rehabilitation farm in Hadley, England. His parents got their free passage to Canada by leading an immigrant party on the boat. Arriving in Toronto, Ontario, with nine children and twenty dollars they spent the first few days in an immigrant shelter. Grandpa Stevens soon got a job in a local bakery and eventually bought a small bakery himself, renaming it "Stevens Bread and Cakes." I have a photograph of the horse-drawn van with which they delivered bread and cakes in Toronto. One day while my father was delivering pastries—can you remember when goods were brought to your door before the invention of delivery drones?—he said to himself, I am not going to do this for the rest of my life. So he started studying at night for his certificate in general accounting. But his background was just above the poverty line. Money was precious. He did not always have it in his heart to say, "It is just money." But over the years we all have passages with respect to our journey with money. He did. Certainly I did and do, as did my mother.

My mother came from a much poorer background. She was born in a fishing outport in eastern Newfoundland, at that time not officially part of Canada. She grew up in an isolated fishing village with no running water, no electricity, no telephone, and no roads. Everything came and went by boat. Hare Bay, Bonavista Bay, was part of a rugged sea coast where her family lived mainly on fish and cabbage, the cabbage being grown in the short summer season on the rocky soil. Her father owned a seventy-foot schooner—a boat where the aft mast is taller than the fore mast. With his sons and relatives he sailed that boat with only a compass and sails (no radar and no engine) up the wild Canadian coast of the north Atlantic to Labrador six months a year to fish in the famous Grand Banks. At that time the Banks teemed with cod fish. My mother would often say that her father was the "head" of the family but in reality her family and other fishing families were matriarchies since the men were six months on the sea and six months in the woods cutting timber. Granddad was home enough, however, to sire twelve children. So the family was actually poor, *though they might not have thought of themselves that way*. Mom would remember that one single orange was a phenomenal Christmas present since the orange was imported by ship from Florida and came through various packers to their outport where local entrepreneurs with simple shops would sell to the community what could not be gotten from the sea or the local scrawny land.

I visited there as a twelve year old and recall how even ice cream came packed in dry ice in well-insulated packages, which was a very special treat. My mother remembers that when an iceberg would float into the bay, they would get in their dories and row out, chipping off the ice to make ice cream, which may explain genetically why I am almost addicted to vanilla ice cream. But in her own way my mother, one of twelve, was entrepreneurial. She was the first in her family to leave the bay and make her way at sixteen years of age hundreds of miles west to Toronto where she got a job as a domestic helper in a wealthy Toronto home, the residence of the family that would later produce a TV anchor on Canadian television. Many years later mother remembers flying to Florida and sitting beside this man and saying, "I know who you are"—after which she said, "I changed your diapers." But it was a poor background. Or was it rich in other ways—self-sufficiency, simple living, attentiveness to creation and the environment, strong family life and community caring and sharing? It is amazing to me how generous my mother was given that she was actually emotionally fragile. But she had many winning characteristics.

She was undoubtedly beautiful and became a Christian in the Salvation Army Corps in Hare Bay as a young girl. My father fell in love with her when he met her in the Toronto Salvation Army Corps. He played the tuba and she was a songster. They married and moved to Montreal to work in a steel fabrication company. Dad had previously had a period of working in the bank. But after each of three births, the middle being born dead, Mom went into a deep depression. Most likely today it would have been diagnosed as post-partum psychosis. My brother John, six years older than me, remembers that when I was two, Dad would be chasing Mom in the second story of our Montreal house to keep her from jumping out of the window. So upon doctor's advice Dad and Mom moved back to Toronto where she had the support of the extended family since by then several Newfoundland immigrants had come there from her outport. It was there that Dad got the chance of his lifetime to head up a division of the company in Toronto, the work which eventually led to his becoming president. They did not have much money at first. But Mom knew how to live on next to nothing, as did Dad. But as the company grew and Dad's salary increased astronomically, this couple with grade three and grade eight education, Mom and Dad respectively, became wealthy. So apart from my earliest years

I grew up in a home of plenty. I drove a big Buick to high school
and had everything I wanted. But Mom never lost her generosity,
never forgot what it was like to be poor. I keep asking where her
generosity came from.

I remember, for instance, how frequently I would come home
from school and one of the pieces of furniture in my bedroom would
be missing: a bed, a dresser or a desk. Mom was furnishing an apartment for one of her nieces, nephews, or cousins, of which there
were just under a hundred, as they came up from the outport in
Newfoundland to work in Toronto, mostly in Dad's factory. The next
day a truck would bring a replacement from Eatons in Toronto.

Rich and Poor Together

When I was a teenager we moved out of north Toronto to a distant
suburb (as it was then) which was a "dog patch": no building code,
no zoning bylaws, no standards for housing and no amenities. Mom
and Dad built a lovely three-bedroom home on three acres of land.
We had an electric pump that drew water from a drilled well, had
a sewage drainage field for indoor plumbing and other amenities.
Down the road was a mansion owned by the person who bought
the Toronto Maple Leafs hockey team. But next door in a tiny lot
up the hill there was a one-room shack with no running water, no
electricity, no central heating or indoor plumbing in which lived a
very old and ailing woman and her fifty-year-old son who cared for
her. They got some social assistance but very little, such as it was
then. But I was also getting some social assistance of another kind
by this living arrangement.

This no-zoning-law situation had one advantage: the rich and
poor were living together. My boyfriends from the neighborhood were
both rich and poor. We had rich in one side and poor on the other.

In winter, when the outside taps in Toronto would normally
freeze and therefore were almost always drained and turned off,

we kept our tap open because Albert Jupp, in the shack up the hill, came twice a day with two pails to get water, one for washing and one for drinking. My mother has to be one of the most generous souls on earth as I have said. She could not sit down to a fine dinner of roast beef, fresh vegetables, roast potatoes, and fresh-baked apple pie with vanilla ice cream—yes it started with her—without thinking about Albert Jupp and his mother. So as a teenager I was pressed into service to carry up the hill, night after night, two plates of cooked food for our poor neighbors next door. I wish I could say I did this with a generous heart. I sometimes resented the task, perhaps partly because it confronted me daily with the truth that I was a rich young man confronting real poverty, real powerlessness, and real hopelessness. I little realized at the time that the rich cannot be saved without the poor. But this nightly pilgrimage was actually a spiritual journey in which I was forced to confront my own existence, my own world that would be a lot easier if I had been insulated from first-hand contact with the poor and powerless. It is easier to send a check than to send ourselves. I was struggling to find out why we do not befriend the poor. Why do we prefer to pay others to feed the hungry, care for orphans, and welcome the stranger? Night after night I was walking through my heart as I walked up the hill. What is it that keeps us in our hermetically sealed containers, silo communities where property values are "protected" through bylaws, and clubs, where we worship in churches made up of people "just like us." We keep schedules so packed that we could not stop to help a person wounded on the roadside lest we be late for some important meeting.

All for Number One

In fact I loved having it all. I had a car, great clothes, girlfriends, a fantastic camera, a hi-fi sound system (do you know what that is?), and on it goes. My father once confronted me with this fact when

I was sixteen. He took me aside when we were outside doing some chores. This is the only occasion in my entire lifetime that I can recall Dad saying something negative about me or to me. "It's all for number one [meaning me], isn't it, Paul?" I cannot say for certain that this was an essential preparatory moment for my embracing the Christian way, which I did in less than two years. I did become a Christian in an odd context. My parents, with their stubborn ill-formed English but fine clothes and big cars, chose to go to a very large and well-heeled church in Toronto. It catered to the "carriage trade," people with expensive cars and lots of money. The ushers wore tuxedos and the choir had five paid soloists. I was baptized that year at sixteen but had no personal relationship with Jesus. But, being entrepreneurial and loving to work with my hands I would sit at the back right pew and design projects I was making in our home shop.

My eye caught the note in the church paper about a youth group meeting Sunday nights. I decided to try it out. It was in the worst possible room for young people: steam pipes, no windows, dirty, with ten people sitting in a circle with long sad faces. I said,

"Hi! I'm Paul Stevens and I am here to join your group."

"That's too bad," they said.

"Why?"

"It's our last meeting," they replied. I inquired why.

"We can't find anyone to be president."

Then they looked at me.

"If you are willing to be president we will keep meeting."

"It's a deal," I said.

So I took over the group on my first meeting. And then I planned and organized, as I assumed church groups should do, Bible studies and prayer meetings. At one of those prayer retreats in a summer camp up north I was apprehended by Jesus and became a Christian. The speaker I hired was hopeless. But God got through to me anyway in waves and waves of liquid love in an hour of complete silence which

I had planned for everyone, including myself. It was devastating, revelatory and a breakthrough all at once. So the next morning, I announced to the group that their president had gotten saved, which created no small stir. But I made an early and crucial discovery.

I suddenly realized that the Christian way is not about religion but about life. That was the beginning of an abrupt change in my attitude toward money, among many things. Up until then I had luxuriated in wealth, loved it. But now I became very critical of my parents and their approach to money. I judged them to be materialistic. Subsequently I have discovered that I was more materialistic than they were! I started to read the story of St. Francis, who grew up in a wealthy home and embraced Lady Poverty, giving it all up. My nightly trip up the hill with two laden dinner plates became more of a personal lifestyle. I spent time in the slums of Hamilton, Ontario, identifying with the poor, loving them and maybe helping them a little. We married and moved into a poor area of Montreal where I was pastor of a struggling and needy church. We had an alcoholic living in the back room and a prostitute sleeping on the sofa in the living room. I spent a lot of time delivering groceries to hungry families, physically moving people from one apartment to another—because they had not been able to pay their rent. I got to know how their bedsteads went together and knew how to assemble personal items. We got the use of a farm in the country to take people from the inner city out on weekends where they could grow some vegetables.

Among the Montreal Poor

During those years Gail, my wife, remembers how little money we had. She would, with our three young children, line up in the supermarket with a trolley of food, anxious as to whether she had enough when she got to the till because we were on a twenty-five-dollar-a-week food budget. She would sweat her way through the line, sometimes having to take some items back. Meanwhile my parents and hers were supportive but more astonished than anything, without fully realizing what was making us tick. They stuck with us through those years of seeing money as a problem and having as little of it as we could manage. That changed in time.

We are all on pilgrimages with respect to money, since we are sometimes influenced by the culture, by advertising, or by the powerfully learned lessons at home. And sometimes we are transformed by hearing a perspective "from the other side" from the revealed Word of God, which we are attempting in this book to share.

With some family help we bought a home in Montreal. "This is how the rich live," said one of the members of our church. I was shocked. Was I indeed rich? Next door was a lawyer family that seemed to have lots of money. They were rich, not us, not me. In time we developed an amazing spiritual friendship with our next-door neighbors with whom we shared vacations and weekly, often nightly, sharing, talking, praying, and reading books together. In time they were drinking very expensive bottles of wine and we were eating chicken soup, but our friendship survived the lifestyle differences. What did not survive was our living next door to them. But our spiritual friendship did survive even though we moved hundreds of miles away. We kept up the relationship until the day our neighbor passed away. Meanwhile I began to pastor a well-to-do church in Vancouver, BC. It was famine to feast.

While I was a student counsellor in the years following Montreal, when we were sometimes out of cash, we had prayed at the dinner table for bread, and amazingly usually a check came through the mail shortly after, or some other serendipity came our way. But in this nice church we thought we had a big salary (it was not actually that big). We were able to buy a piece of land on the ocean and, handy as I am, we built a tiny cottage for our family, largely from construction leftovers. We had money again. But all of that came to an abrupt end.

I left that church and apprenticed as a carpenter mid-life, work-ing for five dollars an hour (with three teenage children, a home, and a car). I worked three jobs, forty hours for a home renovation com-pany, and two weekend jobs, to supply what we needed to survive. On top of that we were leading a small church that reached out to street people and young people that flocked to Vancouver beaches in the summer months. Once again we were steaming headlong toward poverty. But God supplied our needs largely in the shape of work. But I must admit that money had a hold on me. I would lie in bed at night, in those precious moments before you fall asleep, trying to fig-ure out if we had enough to pay the mortgage, the utilities, food, gas for the car, and of course clothing and things for the family. I feared having too little. Later I would fear having too much.

Hammering Nails in Vancouver

I scraped together some money and bought into the business and became an equal partner. This gave me more income, longer work hours but fulfilling work. The nice thing about doing renovation work in homes where the people are still living is that you enter their world and have a privileged inside view of how they live and why. I remember especially so many conversations over coffee and lunch breaks with home owners. On one very low day, low for me as I was struggling with what I was doing, I said to one owner who was a believer, "I think I am wasting my life."

"Never forget," he responded, "that Moses had two useless ca-reers, an administrator in Egypt and a shepherd in Midian. And God made him an administrator and shepherd of the people of God." I have to admit that I was a little encouraged by this but also a little troubled.

I was troubled because in some ways this gave into the old dual-ism that some work, some people, and some places are sacred and others are secular. I had gotten sucked into this when I first became a Christian that weekend in the northern Ontario camp. With the rush of God's love in my heart I wanted nothing more than to serve God "full time." And there was no one in my life at that time who could tell me that I did not have to become a pastor or missionary to serve God "full time." I had not grasped the this-worldly and this-life dimension of being in and working in the kingdom of God. So I entered theological studies and indeed have spent a full two decades of my adult life as a pastor. But I have also spent a decade in business (which turned out to be a full-time service to God and neighbor and a way of "doing the Lord's work") and three decades as a professor. As I look back at age eighty-two I have no regrets for my life path. Indeed as Søren Kierkegaard once said, quoted above, "Life is lived forward but understood backwards."[2] And even when I have made some stupid occupational mistakes, our gracious God has in God's amazing way redeemed those mistakes. There is no "center of God's will"—that elusive bull's-eye in the target that we all try to hit. While there is not a wonderful *plan* for our lives, that construction blueprint which you have to discover and follow slavishly or you will be in deep trouble, there is something better: God has a wonderful *purpose* for our lives, and in this book we are discovering that wonderful purpose in the area of money.

No Retirement for Christians

So here I am now as a so-called retiree. I say "so-called" because I do not believe in retirement and think we should work till we die whether remunerated or not. But of course it is important to leave behind certain high-stress jobs and make room for younger men and women. That's why I retired from the faculty of Regent College eleven years ago. As a former dean I used to get a hundred applications from unemployed PhDs for every open position we had. So I retired but continued to teach more or less full time. I get paid as a "sessional" which means about one-fifth of what the normal professor gets. But that's OK. I don't have a massive pension plan and thankfully have remained in good health and am still at eighty-two "gainfully employed." Sort of.

Two years ago we started the Institute for Marketplace Transformation to assist people worldwide with the integration of faith and work.[3] This book is part of that enterprise. I sometimes get a small allowance for my leadership in that movement. But it is essentially a movement of volunteers. So how do I and my wife live? It is complicated by our view of family stewardship.

In the East children are to care for their parents; in the West parents are to care for their children. I know that's an overstatement but not much. My parents' inheritance came to me at the age of fifty. We essentially passed it on to our three children to enable them to put a down payment on a house for their families. People in the East think we were crazy. It is the duty of children, they say, to look after their parents in their old age. But in the West it is different. There are scriptures in the Bible on both sides of this debate. Jesus railed at the Pharisees who dedicated their money to God (presumably through the temple) and therefore did not have the means to look after their aging parents. Eastern and Asian Christians lean heavily on the injunction in the Ten Commandments to "honor father and mother," which they understand to mean "take care of them," while people in the West understand that to mean give them honor, to esteem them.[4] Second Corinthians puts it in the Western way: "Children should not have to save up for their parents, but parents for their children" (12:14). In some societies the first wins out: providing for and obeying your parents. Often in Africa we find married men obeying their parents and putting their parents before their spouse, with terrible results in the marriage. So in Africa where Gail and I have lived for parts of ten years I often asked church elders, "Should a married man obey his parents?" to which the answer was always, "Yes." I then asked, "If a married man obeys his parents, how can he, in the words of Genesis chapter two, 'leave father and mother' to cleave to his wife?" This usually resulted in silence. So one of the issues we have to wrestle with in this book is stewardship of money within the family. I am thinking as I write this of a friend who is now quite incapacitated and residing in a not-very-nice "seniors" residence. He had been wildly generous with his money and assets through his lifetime, sometimes working for nothing in struggling enterprises. But now he keeps saying over and again, "The only regret I have in my life is that I did not prepare for my support in old age." And his one daughter cannot help.

So here I am as a "retiree" who is working forty or more hours a week (and loving it) trying to figure out "if we have enough money to live until we both die." We have some savings. We have a valuable apartment which we can "eat" (by means of a secured line of credit) when the savings and investments run out—which they will in five years at the present rate, or sooner if I stop working for some re-muneration or get sick.

It's not "just" money as my father once said! Money is impor-tant. It is a complicated reality. It is a grace and gift, and can be a sacrament. But it has a power and can grab hold of our hearts. It is not neutral.

To find out why and how to relate to money we need to ask a fundamental question: what is money anyway? We have to ask how money relates to the meaning of life. We have to explore what money means in the history of the church. We have to ask what Christian stewardship is. And to these crucial questions we now turn. But first we need to explore why money has such a hold on us and to do this we need some history.

3

Holy Money—a Brief History and Why It Is So Complicated to Handle

The magical properties, with which the Egyptian priest-craft anciently imbued the yellow metal, it has never altogether lost.

John Maynard Keynes
on the power of gold[1]

I (Clive) grew up in Asia in the 1960s and 1970s. All our daily necessities were bought at the corner general store. In those days, every neighborhood in Singapore had at least one. The store owner knew almost every customer by name. I remember my mother instructing me to run to the store for cooking oil, salt, and dried food. I would bring the record of accounts kept in a small pocketbook to be updated by the storeowner. Such transactions were all based on trust, just as today we trust the reliability of currencies and the people with whom we are making business transactions. Our account was settled once a month when my father received his monthly wage. A good credit record with the storeowners was crucial to ensure ongoing credit. Customers not known to the storeowner, or who had a poor credit record, had to make payments in cash.

Fifty years later, this practice of keeping accounts is still common in Asia. Together we recently visited a pastor in the south of Jeju Island, South Korea. Delighted with our visit, this pastor took us to a neighboring seafood restaurant to have lunch. At the end of the lunch our host walked to a table strewn with small pocketbooks and picked up his personal booklet. He recorded the date and the number of persons who ate the lunch. It turns out that his family ate at the restaurant regularly, and all their meals are recorded in this book, with costs settled on a monthly basis. This same type of transaction happened in the ancient world. But there was a difference.

Most money in the ancient world circulated through the temple, not through banks, ATMs, and moneylenders. But how did the average ancient Babylonian pay for sundries? Through copper bracelets or lumps of silver. Prices of certain commodities not controlled by the temple fluctuated according to supply and demand. William Goetzmann, an economics historian, suggests that the Babylonians used a silver-based pricing system to record their payments—like a running tab at the local store. This system was tenable only when it was based on a common trust in a record-keeping system and where there was a reputation for honesty. It was, as Goetzmann says, "a setting in which the preponderance of transactions occurred between people who knew each other and interacted with enough frequency to settle accounts."[2] That was long ago. But today?

Some economists argue that money was created to facilitate exchange. Their explanation goes like this: our ancestors started to barter various goods, and the exchanges made their lives easier. It was from these exchanges that money was created as objects that everyone would accept for exchange. The use of money gradually displaced bartering and facilitated efficient exchanges between people. Today, most people see money as a neutral commodity, whether it is a paper note, a coin, or an entry in a bankbook. This is largely encouraged by viewing money as an efficient exchange tool that is neutral. It is how we use money that makes a moral difference.

Anthropologists, on the other hand, believe money was created not for exchange but for use in the temples more than five thousand

years ago in the ancient Near East. Money, they say, originated as a
unit of account kept in the ancient temples. Money, therefore, has
a soul. According to the anthropologists it is not true, as we will
see, that everything started with barter and then moved to money
and finally to a credit system. Money was there at the beginning
even before amounts of silver or gold were weighted out in a bag or
balanced on a scale.

Either way, in this chapter we are going to explore a brief history
of the origin of money, first associated with temples in the ancient
Babylonian culture, and then we will trace some of its development
to the present day.

Money in the Ancient Babylonian Temple

The world's first bankers, over three thousand years ago, were living
in Babylon.[3] In his history of money Glyn Davies mused that the
world's first civilization likely took place more than seven thousand
years ago situated in a warm and fertile plain between the Euphra-
tes and the Tigris Rivers. It was from here that civilization spread
to neighboring regions. There is evidence that as much as five thousand years ago in the ancient city of Uruk in modern Iraq, a city
which at its peak had ten thousand inhabitants, there was a system
of money sophisticated enough to be able to calculate interest.[4]

So the first use of money had a religious context. It was sacred
and set apart.[5] The earliest banks were temples. In early Sumerian
cities in ancient Mesopotamia, the temple was the center of political
and religious life. As people moved into cities, food was to be brought
in from the surrounding farmland. The temples in ancient Babylon,
already political centers, also became the economic centers for the
distribution of food. This is grounded in the belief that the city was
owned by the god of the city. The temple acted on behalf of the god
and controlled the productive land of the city-state. The temple was
the key employer of the city, enlisting thousands of menial laborers

and skilled artisans. The farmers, too, were probably temple employees under the authority of the temple priests and overseers. Grains were deposited and secured in temples before being distributed to the population under the authority of the priests. Of course, there were also bazaars and smaller markets, but the temple served as the central market. The storehouse of the temple acted as a buffer for food when the harvests were poor or when floods ruined the crops. A dramatic example of this is the biblical story of Joseph, who stored the excess grains from the seven fat years of bounty to redistribute them during the seven lean years of famine. All of these transactions required accountants. Enter the scribes.

Scribes kept track of what was being brought into and sent out of the temple storehouses. The deposits in the temples eventually included crops, fruits, cattle, and precious metals. In order to keep track of the vast varieties and quantities of goods, a standard measure based on a quantity of silver was created. A wide variety of goods were measured in units of silver and compared with one another for the purpose of trade and exchange. Such units of precious metal became what we know as money. The temple ensured the consistency and honesty of weight and measurements by using either a balancing scale or a cup to measure the metal. In the Bible this is called "accurate weights" (Prov. 11:1). It is not, as some have said, "fair price," but rather reliable currency. So money allowed goods to be measured and compared with one another for the purpose of trade and exchange. The temple administration thus was able to monitor and control prices to ensure social stability. In this kind of civilization high interest rates were taboo as they led to escalating debts and slavery. Transactions in the silver-based pricing system were recorded in accounts—like a running tab at a local store. And these exchanges were recorded on clay in one of the earliest forms of writing.

So writing from its very beginnings was closely associated with, if not parallel with, the keeping of accounts. The earliest Sumerian numerical accounts consisted of a stroke for units and a simple circular depression for tens. Archaeologists confirm that writing originated as a means of bookkeeping. Most of the thousands of Sumerian cuneiform documents that have been found were financial, since they recorded lists of livestock and agricultural equipment.[6] The reference to the silver shekel in Leviticus 27 is an example of this form of exchange. The standard monetary unit was the silver shekel from as early as 3500 BC. One shekel of silver was equal in weight to one gur, or bushel, of barley. It is out of this economic, literary, and social background that Abraham and his family first appear in the Bible.

Money in Ancient Israel

Abraham is first mentioned in connection with the city of Ur of the Chaldeans (Gen. 11:28). Ur was a harbor town, probably home to 25,000 to 40,000 people with fishermen and maritime traders, as well as farmers and herdsmen.[7] In the 1920s, Sir Leonard Woolley excavated the ancient city of Ur and uncovered homes, shops, schools, and chapels. Abraham grew up there. But eventually Abraham migrated to Haran and then, because of a specific call and initiative from God, he migrated into Palestine, even though he did not know where he was going. Abraham and his nomadic descendants settled there. Eventually, the Bible says, God gave a set of laws to Moses, and this legislation codified the lifestyle of the covenant God had made with his people. Along with many everyday things, this law regulated economic life. So Abraham's descendants, the Hebrews, were instructed not to charge one another interest, although they could lend with interest when dealing with outsiders. But the paramount concern was for the preservation of the community. They were to have no poor. But this concern was not unique to the Israelite community. It had existed long beforehand.

Limitations on interest rates were a vestige of archaic economic life where the priority was the stability of the community. Prices were prescribed in the ancient world by custom and motivated by *communal interests*, not, as they are today, by supply and demand. These were *sacred concerns*, especially because they focused on the community rather than the individual.[8] In modern times, individuals are valued by what they are worth. But among the Israelites, people were valued through money *in a community context and for the sake of the community*. Examples of this are found in the Bible.

In Leviticus 27:1–8 people to be dedicated to the Lord received different values based on their age and gender: a male between twenty and sixty, fifty shekels; a female, thirty shekels; and a child from one month to five years, three to five shekels. These inequities of age and gender leap off the page to modern eyes. But there was grace present in the ancient biblical economic program. For example, if any people making a vow were too poor to pay the specified amount, they were presented to the priest, who would set the value for them "according to what the one making the vow can afford" (Lev. 27:8). This measure of value was administered by the temple because money was sacred. Later in Israel's history, during the beginning of the era of kings, the sacred money in the temple was richly augmented by King David's personal wealth.

Money in the Jerusalem Temple

King David set aside gold and silver, iron, wood, onyx, turquoise, "stones of various colors, and all kinds of fine stone and marble" for his son, Solomon, to build the temple. David personally gave three thousand talents (a measure of weight) of gold from Ophir and seven thousand talents of refined silver for overlaying the walls of the building (1 Chron. 29:2–4). The most holy place of Solomon's Temple alone was lined with cedar from Lebanon and covered with six hundred talents of gold. So the temple was visibly not only a religious center but also an economic powerhouse. And the temple benefited from it.

Devoted worshippers made dedications, tithes, and offerings in the temple. The Hebrews who lived too far away from Jerusalem to bring their animals there to sacrifice for a festival were instructed to convert their bountiful harvest into silver, buy the necessary food and sacrifices at the temple, and celebrate in that location by buying wine and good food for their consumption (Deut. 14:24–26). What an amazing image of the kingdom of God: a party! All of this, however, was gain for the temple, which benefited from the sale of the meat offerings and food needed by the worshippers. Indeed, the biggest income for the temple would have come from the half-shekel temple tribute required of every male Israelite. But the temple also supported the local economy.

Significant numbers of priests and Levites were on the temple's payroll. There were businesses that catered to the visiting worshippers' purchase of meat offerings and businesses that provided food and lodging. Some businesses supplied the temple with its huge requirement of incense, fuel, cloth, cooking vessels, and vessels for carrying blood. The ongoing building and refurbishing of the temple, like a medieval cathedral, created work for local tradespeople. According to Josephus, 18,000 men were put out of work when Herod completed the rebuilding of the temple. But all this made the temple vulnerable.

While the wealth and gold of the temple were the pride of the Jews, the temple became a perpetual magnet for greedy invaders throughout Israel's history. After Solomon's death, Shishak king of Egypt attacked Jerusalem in 925 BC. Shishak was armed with 1,200 chariots and 60,000 horsemen and "innumerable troops of Libyans, Sukkites, and Cushites." Shishak took the fortified cities of Judah and, when he came to Jerusalem, "carried off the treasures of the temple of the Lord" and the gold shields Solomon had made

(2 Chron. 12:9). Under King Joash (2 Chron. 24) and King Josiah (2 Kings 22), the people made generous contributions in rebuilding the temple. However, much of the wealth of the temple was also repeatedly plundered by the Jewish kings willing to pay tribute to threatening foreign powers. King Asa of Judah sent all that was left of the silver and gold to the king of Aram, Ben-Hadad, to break his treaty with Israel and attack Baasha, king of Israel (1 Kings 15:18, 19). King Jehoash of Israel attacked Jerusalem, broke off a six-hundred-foot section of the wall, and "took all the gold and silver and all the articles found in the temple of the LORD and in the treasuries of the royal palace" (2 Kings 14:14). Ahaz stripped all the treasures of the temple and palace as a gift to the king of Assyria (2 Kings 16:8). Ahaz went even further and removed the bronze altar and replaced it with a replica from Damascus (2 Kings 16:10–16). When the king of Assyria threatened Judah, Hezekiah, king of Judah, took three hundred talents of silver and thirty talents of gold from the temple to appease Assyria (2 Kings 18:14–16). So the temple treasury was repeatedly raided and sometimes used as tribute to an invading king in return for peace.

Scripture tells of one very unwise grand tour of the vast temple treasury given to a foreigner. King Hezekiah foolishly arranged an examination of his treasures for his Babylonian visitors. "Hezekiah received the envoys and showed them all that was in his storehouses—the silver, the gold, the spices and the fine olive oil—his armory and everything found among his treasures. There was nothing in his palace or in all his kingdom that Hezekiah did not show them" (2 Kings 20:13). It was all taken away when Jerusalem finally collapsed under the mighty Babylonians. Nebuchadnezzar, the Babylonian king, laid siege to Jerusalem in 587 BC, pillaged the temple, and removed the treasures (2 Kings 25:13–15). During Roman times, the temple in Jerusalem was looted yet once again. Titus, along with Tiberius Julius Alexander, led the Roman army to besiege and conquer the city of Jerusalem, defeating the Judean rebels who

controlled the city in AD 66. The siege ended on August 30 with the
sacking of the city and the destruction of its Second Temple. But
the relation of money to the centers of religious worship existed
not only in the ancient world and in the Hebrew community but
also in Greek civilization.

Money in the Greek Temples

In ancient Greece, the king and his priests made sacrifices on behalf of the whole community. In this context German economist
and historian Bernhard Laum argues from linguistic and archae-
ological evidence that the first use of money as a measure of value
can be traced to these sacrificial practices in classical antiquity.[9]
Money was associated with the portions of a sacrificial bull's flesh
distributed by religious authorities during the rituals of communal sacrificial meals. According to Laum, every festive meal was
a sacrificial one. The beasts were killed and the meat prepared in
order to distribute it among the people in payment for their various services. Each person consumed the meat on the spot under
the observation of a religious authority. The redistributive ritual
ensured a just and equal share for everyone. However, the concept
of "equal" does not mean that each participant was allocated an
equal quantity. The portion of meat one received corresponded to
one's social rank. The "egalitarian principle" was based on what
came to be known as the principle of proportionate or geometrical
equality, as reflected in the philosophy of Pythagoras and Plato. So
by allocating to each his "just" and "equal" share, the rituals fos-
tered the spirit of *koinōnia* (community), giving an appearance of
distributive justice and harmony within a community. Thus a central public authority, the priest, used money as a form of "distributive justice." So, once again, in ancient Greece, the use of money
served the religious and social role of establishing some semblance
of justice and equality.[10]

In the Homeric poems, according to Laum, "royal" gifts or highly expensive gifts were calculated in terms of numbers of oxen. A very precious object, such as a shield, a golden tassel, or a beautiful girl, could have the value of four, nine, twelve, twenty, or a hundred oxen. The bull and the ox were treated as sacred animals, representing, it was thought, an embodiment of Zeus or of the "ox-eyed" Hera. These special gifts were "the apex of wealth, [and] a royal property, inappropriate for market exchange," claims Laum.[11]

John Maynard Keynes, the famed economist, saw the history of civilized money as continuous with the urban revolution with which civilization began. Keynes notes that the magical properties that the ancient Egyptian priests attributed to gold were never altogether lost. Keynes also recognized that the special attraction of gold and silver was due not to any rational considerations but to their symbolic identification with the sun and moon and to the sacred significance of the sun and moon in the astrological theology developed by the earliest civilizations.[12] So, it is now important to ask, where does barter figure in these historical developments? As mentioned above, it is commonly thought that barter preceded the use of money. But such may not be the case.

Before There Was Money There Was Money

The standard economic textbook argument goes like this: Once upon a time, there was barter. It was difficult. There wasn't always someone who wanted what you had to offer. So people invented money. Then came the development of banking and credit. This idea, presented in schools and museums, was commonly accepted. It has been supported by theorists and philosophers and has formed the foundation of much economic thought. But anthropologists argue that the reverse seems true. We created money or a credit system first, more than five thousand years ago. Barter came later, after people became familiar with the use of money as a unit of measure or account.

David Graeber, an anthropologist, is probably best known to the world as the organizer of Occupy Wall Street and the ingenious slogan, "We are the 99%." In chapter two of his bestselling and award-winning book, *Debt: The First 5,000 Years*,[13] Graeber, along with other anthropologists and historians, has criticized the standard economists' theory of money: first barter, then money and credit. Taking the other view—that barter came first—he shows that barter first appears in Aristotle's *Politics*. The direct exchange of commodities, Aristotle argued, is natural and satisfies the natural requirement of sufficiency. Natural exchange is based on the right to property. Aristotle saw barter as the natural outcome of specialization that led to increase in production beyond the needs of any one household. These surpluses encouraged households to exchange their excess commodities with other items that they needed. Then in 1776, Adam Smith, a professor of moral philosophy at Glasgow who is often considered the father of economics, took Aristotle's view further.

Here is what Adam Smith said:

> The butcher has more meat in his shop than he himself can consume, and the brewer and the baker would each of them be willing to purchase a part of it. But they have nothing to offer in exchange, except the different productions of their respective trades, and the butcher is already provided with all the bread and beer which he has immediate occasion for.[14]

So, argues Smith in *The Wealth of Nations*, the butcher "supplies the far greater part of them by exchanging that surplus part of the produce of his own labor, which is over and above his own consumption. . . . Every man thus lives by exchanging, or becomes, in some measure, a merchant, and the society itself grows to be what is properly a commercial society."[15] Only human beings, Smith argues, have this passion to "truck, barter, and exchange one thing for another." But through all the research, no such fabled land of barter has been found!

Witness explorers and missionaries. Around the nineteenth century many missionaries, adventurers, and colonial administrators moved out into the world, carrying along Smith's book, expecting to find a land of barter. None ever did. Many different economic systems were found by historians and anthropologists but not a single one of them was a pure barter economy. Caroline Humphrey's definitive anthropological work on barter concludes: "No example of a barter economy, pure and simple, has ever been described, let alone the emergence from it of money; all available ethnography suggests that there never has been such a thing."[16]

In reviewing native cultures from Brazil, the Gunwinggu people of western Arnhem Land in Australia, and the Pukhtun of Northern Pakistan, Graeber argues that in a community where everyone lives together and cares for one another there is a desire to deal fairly and honestly with one another. Even if things are swapped, they are likely to be considered gifts for one another. In contrast, "swapping one thing directly for another while trying to get the best deal one can out of the transaction is, ordinarily, how one deals with people one doesn't care about and doesn't expect to see again."[17]

The standard economic textbook argument that we started with barter, then created money—nails, shells, fish, tobacco, or anything of value—to replace cumbersome barter, and then eventually we developed credit systems seems not to be true. Anthropologists believe the reverse is true. We created virtual money or credit systems first, more than five thousand years ago. Barter is not actually an ancient phenomenon. Indeed, it became widespread in modern times after people became familiar with the use of money. During the collapse of the ruble in Russia in the 1990s and of the dollar in Argentina around 2002, elaborate systems of barter cropped up.[18] In the years after *The Wealth of Nations* was published, scholars discovered that most of the examples of commodities, like fish, nails, shells, and tobacco, that were used as money were used by people familiar with the use of money as a unit of account or a unit of value.

The Soul of Money

We have seen that money as a measure of value has a long history, probably longer even than barter. Physical objects, such as conch shells or tobacco, were used as a measure of value. This was money. But where there were precious metals, especially silver and gold, these became the preferred units of money. But this measurement of value was never quite neutral.

Money, since its beginning, has been a spiritual matter and was created within the temple for the sacred management of the temple. The earliest use of money was within a canopy of sacredness to moderate the wealth of the temple and to justly distribute goods among the residents of the city. Like all the "principalities and powers" named in the Bible (Eph. 6:12), money has a dark spiritual side. As we saw in the temple context, money demands devotion, devotion that should be rendered to God himself.

So, not surprisingly, Jesus often used the word *mammon* or "unrighteous money" for this medium of exchange that most people think is neutral. The English word *mammon* derives from an Aramaic word that has the same root as the word *Amen*, the affirmation with which people often close their prayers saying, in effect, "Let it be secure." And many people do seek their final security in money. "The almighty dollar" is a strangely evocative term in everyday speech, hinting that money can easily become godlike, offering solace, help, and even salvation. The story of how we can deliver money from its insidious tendency to pull on our heart strings for security and power, and, at the same time, how we can transform money so we can serve Caesar (that is, our earthly obligations and neighbors) and serve God *at the same time* takes us to the New Testament and the revolutionary ministry of Jesus. He smashed the sacred-secular dualism that plagues people of faith today globally. To that we now turn.

4

Giving to God and Caesar—
the Complicated End of Dualism

*"Render unto Caesar that which is Caesar's, and unto
God that which is God's." In my opinion, the entire problem of life in contemporary culture can be defined as
the challenge to understand that saying of Jesus.*

Jacob Needleman[1]

It is not easy to unravel this complicated saying. It reveals a dilemma, a dilemma that was exposed in the last chapter. There we
explored the history of how money originated and became connected with temples. It had a sacred context. And through this association and because it has become one of the principalities and
powers—sometimes being called mammon—we discovered that
money is not neutral. This, however, does not mean that this sacred
association guarantees that the ways we make and handle money
are part of our whole spiritual life as members of the kingdom of
God on earth. And so we turn to this astonishing word of Jesus in
the Gospel of Matthew. Here he is not simply inviting us to decide
first, what is worldly or secular—"giving to Caesar" (and therefore
our this-worldly duties)—and then second, what is sacred—"giving
to God" (such as using money for the support of stated Christian
ministry and the church, or other ways of making a religious and
God-pleasing use of money). That division between secular and sacred can be described as a dualism, a division which has plagued

the church for centuries. Reading the newspaper is secular; reading
the Bible is sacred. Being in business is secular; being on a church
committee is sacred. Eating a meal is secular; receiving the Lord's
Supper is sacred. Building a house is secular; building a church is
sacred. But that is not all.

This dualism has driven women and men to seek what they think
are the highest vocational roles as monks, nuns, priests, or pastors,
occupations that are innately holy and especially pleasing to God. You
have seen how we both were influenced by this in our early years. Such
dualism relegates money to the realm of "this world" without reference to God's purposes and the possible holy use of money. Worse still,
this insidious dualism has led to a two-level spirituality summarized
by an early Christian historian, Eusebius of Caesarea (about AD 315),
who said there are two ways of life. "The one is spiritual and dedicated
to contemplation." Those following this perfect life are devoted solely
to the service of God and "in mind and spirit have passed to heaven."
The other way is more human and in it people do farming and trade
"as well as religion." Then comes his soul-crushing conclusion: "A *kind
of secondary grade of piety* is attributed to such people."[2] Jesus was
addressing this dualism in the passage we are studying.

Jesus and Dualism

Palestine was occupied by the Roman government. A special tax
imposed on non-Roman citizens was known as Caesar's tax. Direct Roman taxation had sparked the revolt of Judas of Galilee in
AD 6, and this insurrection was brutally crushed with revolution-
aries being executed on crosses in the countryside. This happened
when Jesus was a boy. The resistance movement continued under
the general title of the Zealots. Caesar's tax was hated.[3] Nationalists
favored outright rebellion or at least passive resistance. Jesus was a
person of the world. The incarnation—God becoming human—was
total. God went through a complete human experience from con-

ception to resurrection. The Word became flesh culturally, socially, spiritually, geographically, and politically.

But in this case, in an occupied country, Jesus was being set up. Matthew 22:15–22 tells us that the Pharisees, fundamentalist Jews, and the Herodians, those indirectly in league with the occupying power, sent their followers to test Jesus. They "buttered him up" with compliments. They told him that he was a person of integrity, that he was not swayed by people's opinions, that he taught the way of God according to the truth, and that he was not influenced by the position people held in society. This, however, was his reputation. Then came the bombshell: "Is it right to pay the imperial tax to Caesar or not" (v. 17)? The question put Jesus in a bind.

If Jesus refused to pay the tax, he would satisfy the Israeli nationalists but would supply convenient proof of his treasonable attitude, which would be useful in persuading the Roman government to dispense with him.[4] N. T. Wright says that the question raised comes with a health warning. "Tell people they should not pay, and you might end up on a cross."[5] If, on the other hand, he paid the tax he would forfeit some of his following as he had tacitly sided with Rome. He would also denigrate money to something that operates only in the secular realm. The Roman denarius was an offensive coin to Jews because it had the image of Caesar on it, and Jews were forbidden to make images of people. This was especially so in the case of Caesar, who was described as a "son of a god."[6] For normal commerce the Romans had minted copper coins without the image of Caesar on it in deference to the Jews. Nothing could have prepared Jesus's questioners for his response.

His response was vehement, almost verbal violence. He called them "hypocrites," one of the most terrible accusations that can be made of someone, since it touches what we claim to hold most dear, our faith and our values. Then he asked for a coin and requested that they state whose image was on it. Ancient coins usually had two sides, one of which had a divine character, a god, or a Caesar-

god, and the other side a secular symbol. American money even
has written on it, "In God We Trust" on one side. The Canadian
Toonie (two-dollar coin) has an image of the Queen of England on
one side and a Canadian black bear on the other. In this case, the
fact that Jesus's questioners had one of the image-bearing coins
"cut the ground from under their feet." R. T. France suggests, "They
were using Caesar's money, so let them also pay his taxes!"[7] So Jesus
concluded, "Give back to Caesar what is Caesar's, and to God what
is God's" (v. 21). What was Jesus doing?

Jesus was not suggesting, as is commonly practiced in Christianity today, that ten percent of our money goes to the church (this is
"giving to God what is God's"), thirty percent (more or less) is paid
to Caesar or the current government in taxes, and the rest is ours.
This separates the holy use of money from the secular use, which
is the insidious dualism that reigns almost everywhere today.

In this extraordinary incident Jesus asserted that money can
have a holy purpose. He fulfilled the desire to meet a divine purpose
and this-worldly obligations *at the same time.* And teasingly, he left
open the question of what "giving to God" means. To get behind
this we must examine the influence of the Old Testament, the surrounding Greek culture, and the development of a growing dualism
of sacred-secular in the history of the West and East, all factors in
the dualism found even in the church today.

The Old Testament Factor

Under the old covenant, the Hebrew people had to learn to distin-
guish between the ordinary and the holy. For example, "This is a
lasting ordinance for the generations to come, so that you can dis-
tinguish between the holy and the common . . ." (Lev. 10:10). The law
established holy places (the tabernacle, the temple, holy Mount Si-
nai), holy acts (festivals, offerings, worship) and holy people (prophets, priests, and princes). But God has done something new in the

coming of Christ, ordaining the priesthood of all believers (1 Pet.
2:5), the prophethood of all believers (Acts 2:17), and the princely
rule of all believers (Rev. 22:5).[8] Holiness is not separating ourselves
from our this-worldly life in matters such as handling money. Holiness is dedicating everything to God and God's purposes. This is the
radical message of the New Testament, the message of the kingdom
of God, as we see in Romans.

In Romans 12:1–2 the apostle Paul bids us present our entire
bodily life to God as "a living sacrifice," as this is our "true and proper
worship." This means one hundred percent of life is dedicated to God
and God's purposes, including all our seemingly "secular" obligations.
It is astonishing that the New Testament never says that first-century
Christians went to worship services. They were worshipping all week
long. They gathered for mutual edification.[9] Why did they refuse to
separate life into "silos"? Because Jesus the carpenter-entrepreneur
smashed the old dualism and introduced a way of life in which all was
holy, from tilling the soil to trading on the stock exchange, albeit often, if not always, mixed with sin and deconstruction in this life. There
is no "secondary grade of piety" attached to being a businessperson,
homemaker, artist, ditch-digger, or banker. And from time to time,
this life-transforming perspective has been rediscovered against the
force of gravity that keeps pulling people back into dualistic thinking
and living. But it is fragile. Indeed, Needleman concludes, "It is inevi-
table that religion becomes worldly under the pretext of making the
worldly life religious."[10] In due course we will unpack these words, for
this is exactly what happened. One influence on the demise of this
radical synthesis of life, all of it including the use of money, came from
the surrounding Greek culture.

The Greek Philosophical Factor

In the Greek world the body was considered the shell, generally an
evil covering, for a precious immortal soul. Salvation was getting

the soul out of the body. Death was a friend as it liberated people from the prison of physical life. The future, for the Greek world, was the immortality of the soul. In contrast, the Christian hope is not the immortality of the soul but the resurrection of the body, whole-person transfiguration in a new heaven and new earth.

But this view of the human person, higher and lower, that Greek culture generally envisioned was like a thick fog surrounding a city, permeating the thought life and spirituality of early Christians.[11] Plotinus, the single most influential philosopher of the ancient world, and one who profoundly influenced Augustine and Western Christianity, stated in a classic way the great opposites of spirituality and materialism.

> The pleasure demanded for the Sage's life cannot be in the enjoyments of the licentious or in any gratifications of the body.... Let the earth-bound man be handsome and powerful and rich, and so apt to this world that he may rule the entire human race: still there can be no envying of him, the fool of such lures.

The Sage, in contrast, will wear away the "tyranny of the body . . . by inattention to its claims."[12] Trade for Aristotle was essentially suspicious if not downright perverted. "Anybody who does anything for pay is by nature not a truly free person."[13]

Most of the early church fathers took on this "upper and lower" approach to life: the higher for the monk, nun, and priest and the lower for the person who works in the world. This became incarnated in the supremacy of medieval monasticism which was considered the way of Mary over and against the way of Martha (Luke 10:38–42). As a result, by the fifteenth century only the monk, nun, and priest were regarded as having a calling. Karl Barth's summary is apt: "According to the view prevalent at the height of the Middle Ages [secular work] only existed to free for the work of their profession those who were totally and exclusively occupied in rendering true obedience for the salvation of each and all."[14] This is not far from the contemporary idea that business people in the church are "walking check books" needed to support the pastor.[15] But what they do to make this money is not sacred. So what happened?

The Partial Reformation Factor

In the Protestant Reformation of the sixteenth century Martin Luther reacted to medieval dualism's conclusion that to be converted was to join the monastery. Luther said,

> Therefore I advise no one to enter any religious order or the priesthood, indeed, I advise everyone against it—unless he is forearmed with this knowledge and understands that the works of monks and priests, however holy and arduous they may be, do not differ one wit in the sight of God from the works of the rustic laborer in the field or the woman going about.[16]

But in reacting against monasticism as a kind of salvation machine, Luther unwittingly and unintentionally contributed to the radical secularization of life found in most of the West today.

The story of this is ably recounted in Craig Gay's *The Way of the (Modern) World.* He explores the well-worn writing of Max Weber to illuminate this process.[17] Calvinism, Weber affirmed, taught that some are elected to be saved and others to be damned. This ratcheted up the believer's anxiety level. Previously, one who seriously wanted to prove that he was among the elect would go to the monastery. Now that the monastery door was slammed shut by the Reformers, the only place to prove one's election was in one's worldly calling. But Calvinism taught thrift, that you do not spend everything you make by zealous work in the world. This "worldly asceticism," Weber argues, is exactly the situation needed for capitalism to thrive. His analysis is largely, though not completely, true. Gianfranco Poggi puts it this way, "Only a religious vision that turns worldly reality into a field of experimentation, and the individual into a 'tensed-up being,' relentlessly working that field in the pursuit of a dynamic design, could plausibly be said to have offered such an inspiration."[18]

According to Weber, this is what Calvinism supplied; not the Calvinism taught by the Reformers but the reception of that teaching by what he calls "the lay practitioners of religion."[19] Poggi's conclusion is apt: Weber's argument is partial (addressing a distinctive part of a large historical problem), complex ("it comprises a number of discrete points, connected by a correspondingly high number of steps or transitions") and *momentous*.[20] Weber's thesis is hard to verify empirically but, as the British economist Brian Griffiths notes, "The Protestant ethic thesis turns out to be a specific example of a far more general thesis: namely that the economic process is related in an important way to cultural and religious values."[21]

Commenting on this, Gay offers two possible explanations for the contemporary situation. Either practical rationality (the process of making decisions not by custom and tradition but by calculable and practical outcomes) has somehow received divine and religious sanction, or the religious understanding of life has become "debunked and disenchanted" to give free rein to "pragmatism and egoism." In fact, the second has come out of the first, namely that the sanctioning of practical reason and worldly asceticism led to the disenchanting of everyday activities such as work and making money.[22] Ironically, as Gay puts it, "Christianity appears to be largely responsible for its own demise in the modern period."[23] Money is central to this process.

With the disenchantment of work and exchange, money makes rational calculation and accounting possible but it does this by reducing everything to "mere quantities."[24] This is something that the German social philosopher Georg Simmel elaborated in his massive volume.[25] So, as is said of some merchants, they know the price of everything but the value of nothing.[26]

With later Puritans, things go a notch further. Early Puritans, such as William Perkins, saw both work and ministry above the secular line, placing them in the realm of the sacred entirely encompassed within God's call that comes to everyone. Each person has a particular and holy calling. Perkins describes it this way: "The execution of some particular office, arising of that distinction which God makes between man and man in every society"[27]—the magistrate as he governs his people, the minister in teaching his people, the physician in bringing health, the master in governing his family, the merchant in his business, etc. All callings are for the common good and are holy. "Adam as soon as he was created, even in his integrity, had a personal calling assigned to him by God, which was to dress and keep the garden."[28] And therefore "all who descend from Adam must need to have some calling to walk in, either public, or private, whether it be in the church, or commonwealth, or family."[29] You will note there is no distinction in holiness or "being called" between the minister-pastor and the tradesperson. This is in contrast with Calvin who unwittingly assigned to the Protestant preacher a unique "secret" call and attributed to the Protestant preacher proclaiming the "Christ event" in the preached Word an aura of holiness previously associated with the celebration of the mass in the Catholic tradition.[30] So the slide had begun. And later Puritans lost the synthesis.

R. H. Tawney's study, *Religion and the Rise of Capitalism*, documents the slide. "Plunged in the cleansing waters of later Puritanism, the qualities which less enlightened ages had denounced as social vices emerged as economic virtues."[31] So the Western Christian movement drifted, without the intention of the Reformers, from a largely destroyed dualism to a Deistic, secularized, this-worldly religion attempting to make this-worldly improvements. A former theology professor at Regent College, Klaus Bochmuehl, judged that this arose from an overemphasis on the importance of the so-called "civil" vocation for Christian faith and life.[32] Meanwhile, the Catholic Church continued with the largely sacred-secular divide until Vatican II which, remarkably, ushered in a wealth of perspective, resources, and practical integrations of faith and life, which the National Center for the Laity in Chicago continues to catalog.[33] Ironically, the editor of their journal quotes a zinger from Cardinal Francis George, OMI, that "Everyone in the U.S. is Protestant, including Catholics." By this he means, even Catholics now treasure individual rather than social rights and believe the road to upward mobility is paved with hard work.[34]

So, in the West we have a largely secularized Christianity with substantial elements of the old dualism. Certain activities and services are holy, while dealing with filthy lucre is just what we have to do to maintain our life in the world. And this largely dualistic version of Christianity has been brought to the world through the global mission of the church. Of course, there were exceptions. And parts of the world come under other influences.

The Eastern Religion and Philosophy Factor

While the East cannot be dealt with as a single homogenous whole, certain influences have made dualism even more extreme in the East than in the West. Not all missionaries, of course, carried this dualism in their hearts and tongues. Early Catholic missionaries in China took their place in the court and were teachers of mathematics and science. But in general, their message was a two-level spirituality. If you are truly serious about following Jesus, you will become a missionary or a pastor. This was exacerbated by three additional influences: shamanism, Buddhism, and Confucianism. This is especially true in one country.

Korean Christianity is arguably the most dualistic in Asia. In his study of Korean Christianity, Paul Cho notes that "from its beginning, Korea was a country defined by its passion for religions."[35] Shamanism, belief in an unseen world of gods, demons, and ancestral spirits, is one of the major influences. One striking characteristic of Korea's shamanism, Cho notes, is the "ranking of gods into different categories. The head of all the gods is known as 'Hanamim,' which Koreans considered the Supreme Being with no accessibility."[36] Then, below, there are other gods that serve as "the bridge to the transcendent deity within this system."[37]

So, Cho argues, shamanism has played a major role in the formation of pastoral identity in Korea and the Christianity they proclaim. Many of today's Korean pastors' behaviors resemble much of shamans' behaviors. Such tendency to elevate pastors as more sacred people is well captured in the constitution of the Presbyterian Church of Korea (PCK), regarding how the Lord's Supper ritual should be carried out only by ordained pastors. They are viewed as supernatural people who have the special ability to intercede with God.

A second influence is Buddhism. Essentially, Buddhism is a practical philosophy on how to deal with suffering. By following an eight-fold path of wisdom, ethical conduct, and mental discipline one can attain nirvana, which is the "end of suffering."[38] These disciplines enable a person to disengage from the world. Pastoral identity in Korea, Cho argues again, has been profoundly influenced by this. Essentially, pastors are monks who have given up worldly enterprises, sometimes highly remunerated professions, to devote themselves to attain holiness and to be God's servants. In harmony with Buddhism, Korean pastors preach a lot about the afterlife, where there will be no pain or sufferings. Young-hoon Lee advises, "Christian eschatology includes in itself the danger of denying the present life and over-emphasizing the other world."[39]

And there is a third major influence—Confucianism. Throughout Asia, Confucianism is a powerful influence on family, relationships, and business. It is essentially a philosophy inculcating loyalty, filial piety, benevolence, and trust. Its aim is to create harmony in human relationships. But it does this through a hierarchical ordering of people with appropriate roles and obligations between people: sovereign and subject, father and son, husband and wife, senior and junior, friend and friend. It is widely acknowledged that especially in Korean Christianity Confucian culture dominates. "Leadership is sometimes too authoritarian. The elevated status of pastors hinders biblical servant-leadership, promotes division and personality cults, and stunts discipleship," says Jason Mandryk in *Operation World*.[40] In contrast, biblical Christianity proclaims that the material world is good and that engaging in enterprise (and handling money) can be a calling of God equal to that of the pastor.

In summary, the dualism that persists globally among Christian people has multiple sources: the persistence of Old Testament patterns, the Greek philosophical influence, the decline of the holiness of everyday life following the Protestant Reformation, and the influence of other faiths and philosophies.

So how then do we reconcile both sides of the coin, God and Caesar? How can we give to Caesar what is Caesar's and to God what is God's? This can happen only with a thoroughgoing integration of faith and life. R. T. France, commenting on Matthew 22:15–22, suggests that "this is not the rigid division of life into the 'sacred' and the 'secular', but rather a recognition that the 'secular' finds its proper place within the overriding claim of the 'sacred'."[41] The single or sound eye, Jesus once said (using the eye as a metaphor for faith), means that the whole of the body will be full of light (Luke 11:34–36). In this case money can become a sacrament, a gift, and a grace. But that does not mean deifying money. Jesus deals with mammonism (deifying money) by inviting people to enter a different worldview, the kingdom worldview in which all of life is holy.[42] Scripture shows that money mixes the material with the spiritual grace, an instrument of what we can do simultaneously in the material and spiritual realms. God and Caesar—not separated and not merged but, when it comes to money, all for God since it is God's money anyway. The results of this can be a re-energizing of the kingdom mission of the people of God.

We started this chapter with a quotation from Jacob Needleman commenting on the words of Jesus about giving back to Caesar and to God. Needleman truly said, "In my opinion, the entire problem of life in contemporary culture can be defined as the challenge to understand that saying of Jesus." But that leaves us with a question. Can that nondualistic integration of "giving back to Caesar what is Caesar's, and to God what is God's" at the same time function in a world largely dominated today by democratic capitalism? Put differently, what if "Caesar" today is the capitalist system?

5

Grappling Shrewdly with Capitalism

*Basically, money has become one of the most impor-
tant "measures" in the determination of "value" in the
contemporary world. . . . Money, like the mechanical
clock, is one of the key instruments of the modern age.*

Craig Gay, *Cash Values*[1]

In the last chapter we explored how it is possible to give to Caesar
and to God, to meet our this-worldly obligations and our heavenly
obligations at the same time. We argued that this is implicit in the
teaching of Jesus, especially his central message of the kingdom of
God. But we ended with an intriguing question. In our twenty-first-
century context, what if "Caesar" is the capitalist system itself, or
our work in the capitalist enterprise, or how we use money in a capitalist economy? Put differently, can our work in a highly monetized
economic system such as capitalism contribute in some way to the
kingdom of God, that inbreaking of shalom and human flourishing
that was embodied in Christ himself? And, certainly, the system is
highly monetized, from toothpaste to televisions, from dental floss
to destroyers, from sex to satellites. To grapple with that we must
first understand capitalism, to which we now turn, and in particular, we look at how money has lost its spiritual role even while
claiming an almost godlike loyalty and worship.

The Emergence of Capitalism

In ancient civilizations, such as Mesopotamia and Greece, money
was developed in temples to ensure distributive justice among
the people living in the community through keeping accounts.
This spiritual and social role of money was gradually diluted,
over time, into capitalism in the form of the market economy. Indeed, a cataclysmic shift in economic focus took place during the
mid-19th century, being influenced by the Industrial Revolution.
Through several steps, eighteenth-century capitalism underwent
a radical change: economic behavior became separated from ethics and human values. The economic machine was supposed to
function as an autonomous entity, independent of human needs
and human will. It developed a "contempt for nature—as well as
for all things not machine-made and for all people who are not
machine makers," says sociologist Erich Fromm.[2] Not only was
the system able to run by itself but it also did so according to its
own laws. So various measuring and operating devices had to
be created.

Eighty years ago, an economist at the National Bureau of Economic Research in the United States created the concept of gross
domestic product (GDP) in his report to the US Congress. The GDP
measures the value of economic activity within a country during
a period of one year. GDP is the market value in dollars of all final
goods and services produced in a single economy. Following the
creation of international financial institutions such as the World
Bank and the International Monetary Fund, GDP became the standard measurement for a country's economy. All human activities
under the sun could now be measured in economic terms. And
money is the ultimate standard by which all human progress is
measured. Economies scramble to compete against one another
based on GDP.

Capitalism is a social economic system with several bases:

1. Individual rights, including property rights
2. The rule of law especially regarding business and property
3. Vigorous and competitive private ownership
4. Restrained government interference, so that under capitalism the state gets separated from the realm of economics in the same way as the state gets separated from religion
5. A mechanism for credit creation through the issuance of notes and bills, which is the critical source of dynamism in the system of capitalism[3]

Capitalism has become the prevalent system throughout the Western world today. Starting in Europe, it spread to the United States and then, within the last hundred years, to the Far East and Africa. In the last four decades, communistic or socialistic economies have moved toward open and market-driven policies, as their experiments with collectivism and central planning delivered less than desired economic results. China was transformed from central planning and evolved quickly to embrace a market economy over the decades[4] and is today a unique combination of patriarchal control and Western-style capitalism. The Chinese version has sometimes been called Confucian capitalism or State capitalism. In Europe, on November 9, 1989, the East German Communist Party announced that citizens of the German Democratic Republic, or East Germany, could cross the infamous Berlin Wall[5] that divided East and West whenever they pleased. That night, the last major barrier to capitalism collapsed as East and West Germany worked toward an integrated capitalistic economy.

Astonishing Productivity and the Problem of Capitalism

In his book *The Capitalist Revolution*, Peter Berger observes that "advanced industrial capitalism has generated, and continues to generate, the highest material standard of living for large masses of people in human history."[6] Millions of the poor have been lifted out of grinding poverty, as was proposed by Lord Brian Griffiths in *The Creation of Wealth: A Christian's Defense of Capitalism.*[7]

Craig Gay contends that the astonishing productivity of capitalism places Christians in a dilemma. This growth has brought a negative effect in enlarging the gap between rich and poor—the rich man and Lazarus writ large as in Luke 16:19–31 (to be discussed in the next chapter). This is especially so because modern capitalism is "historically the product of a Christian civilization."[8] To contrast the period of emerging global capitalism with the situation today, take, for example, Paul's late father. As a corporate president just after World War II, he earned five times the amount of the entry-level employees. But today the Chief Executive Officers (CEOs) of the largest 350 firms in the United States earn more than three hundred times the salary of the average employee.[9] Asia is also drawn into this rich-poor gap. In Singapore, an international commerce and financial city, this wage gap is about a hundred times and expanding rapidly. It is widely known that a few people in the world and some companies earn more than whole nations. But this is not the only challenge.

The pervasive use of money in capitalist systems encourages a nonjudgmental stance on moral values. Money flattens all values and makes all decisions and objects comparable on a monetary basis. At the same time, market reasoning is based on freedom and maximizing welfare or social utility. Utilitarianism[10] argues that market exchanges benefit buyers and sellers alike, thereby improving our collective well-being or social utility. Michael Sandel observes:

> Our reluctance to engage in moral and spiritual argument, together with our embrace of markets, has exacted a heavy price: it has drained public discourse of moral and civic energy, and contributed to the technocratic, managerial politics that afflicts many societies today.[11]

We corrupt a good, whether an activity or a social practice, whenever we treat it according to a lower norm than is appropriate for it. For example, having babies in order to sell them for profit is a corruption of parenthood, because it treats children as things to be used rather than beings to be loved. Economists, political scientists, and legal scholars debate this potent image of human life as rational behavior according to economic values, thereby bypassing human values. Rationality, implicit in the capitalist system, often counters our social norms, customs, and traditions.

In short, market reasoning is not complete without moral reasoning. Are all goods available for sale? Should we shoot endangered species for a fee, or worse, buy a human organ because we are sick and have the money? When we corrupt a good or service with money, we destroy its unique characteristics and flatten the quality of the good or service to become an impersonal object that is valueless. From where does this shrewd rationality come?

Lust for money is not the only thing. But it is the main thing. As Adam Smith argued in *The Wealth of Nations,*

> The capitalist project is *not* animated by a search for methods of institutionally liberating the inner drives of every man *in the interest of moral will*. It is animated by a search for methods of institutionally liberating every man's natural instinct of self-preservation in the interest of [a] ... peaceful prosperous life for mankind as a whole.[12]

Would that the capitalist project was for "mankind as a whole," that is, for the benefit of others, everyone on the planet. It is true, however, that, by and large, international trade has built friendship bridges between nations. Japan, for example, would not today bomb its best trading partner, the USA. And William Carey, often called the pioneer of modern missions, argued that now that we have the mariner's compass there is no excuse for not going across the big seas (Atlantic and Pacific) for trade, and while people are doing trade, the good news of the kingdom of God could traverse the globe.[13] Further, Kim Tan is right to argue that enterprise, not aid, is the best way to fight poverty.[14] Why? Because tax-paying companies help the government to build infrastructure and to improve education and health care. In the process, sizable capitalistic and profit-making ventures (for which investors can be found) give people marketable skills and the dignity that is gained through working. But the problem remains.

When Capitalism Becomes a Religion

The sources of all this productivity are, amazingly, partly rooted in the Christian faith. Max Weber, the early twentieth-century sociologist, observes that modern capitalism flourished especially in countries such as the United States and United Kingdom, where "ascetic" forms of Protestantism were important. We explored the impact of this in the last chapter. This "spirit" of capitalism is irrational and unnatural and could not have arisen without the support and sanction of the rational ethics of "ascetic" Protestantism. But these economic successes came only after the purely religious enthusiasm was past, which left in its place a *bourgeois* economic ethic with little or no religious motivation. What started as a good conscience in the legal acquisition of money eventually morphed for many into an insatiable love of money. The trinity of unlimited production, absolute freedom, and unrestricted happiness formed the nucleus of a new religion, which could be called "Progress," and a new heaven, the "Earthly City of Progress" which would replace the City of God. This new religion provided its believers with energy, vitality, and hope. This becomes evident through a comparison of Christian beliefs and the institutions of capitalism.

CHRISTIANITY	CAPITALISM
Eternal salvation	Material well-being
Sins	Market failures
Humans as sinners	Humans as rational
Holy Trinity	Land, labor, and capital
Love, faith, and hope	Self-interest, freedom, and happiness
Discipleship of all nations	Global free-market evangelism
The priesthood	Economists, politicians, wealthy industrialists
Church	Federal Reserve Banks

Capitalism is, for many, a religion for the here and now. The market system promises tremendous economic benefits and happiness. And for good reason.

Gracious Capitalism

As we have seen, the most important contribution of capitalism is not economic progress but the improvement of the quality of lives that this wealth enables. With the rise of capitalism, infant mortality plunged to record lows. Malnutrition and related diseases were brought under control, along with lower incidences of plagues. Consequently, people are, generally, living longer and better. "The good old days" before capitalism were not so good.

By and large, the life of our ancestors was wretched. My (Clive) grandparents lived a hard life raising pigs and chickens in their small farm. There was always so much to do and little time for rest or leisure. They lived in a humble home with a dirt floor until they moved into a small government apartment, which they did when they were no longer able to work. We romanticize the past in literature, poetry, romance, and legends with people who were larger

than life heroes or heroines. The masses living in poverty were a
passing backdrop. Prior to 1400, life expectancy at birth was twenty
to thirty years. Since 1800, life spans have doubled again, largely due
to improvements in environment, food, and medicine that mini-
mized mortality at earlier ages. In the national data for England and
Wales of 1861, for example, infections caused 25 percent of female
deaths before age forty. Almost all deaths before age five were due
to infections.[15] Even as recently as 1921, countries like Canada still
had an infant mortality rate of about 10 percent, meaning one out
of every ten babies did not survive. Michael Novak, probably the
most significant marketplace theologian alive today, notes that "Of
all the systems of political economy which have shaped our history, none has so revolutionized ordinary expectations of human
life—lengthened the life span, made the elimination of poverty and
famine thinkable, enlarged the range of human choice—as has democratic capitalism."[16] And how did this happen?

It was a combination of rational and experimental use of economic organization and technology to satisfy human wants, conclude Rosenberg and Birdzell in their book *How the West Grew
Rich*.[17] From the middle ages, religious and political restrictions
were gradually relaxed and allowed these experiments to be carried
out with ample rewards. Initial autonomy given by political and
religious authorities gave space to experiment. For the economy
to grow, rulers had to sacrifice control and risk losing power. Until
the middle ages, most societies were unwilling to take this risk. This
freedom in experimentation increased in Western societies and led
to extraordinary human flourishing, albeit mixed with lots of deconstruction. But the result was essentially positive.

Jonathan Haidt, social psychologist at New York University's
Stern School of Business, believes that rising prosperity makes
people more open and affirming of social and gender diversities
and environmental challenges.[18] According to Haidt, the best research is from the World Values Survey (WVS) led by Ron Ingle-

hart and Christian Welzel.[19] These authors have surveyed one hundred countries from 1981 to 2014. They asked more than a hundred questions on topics such as religion, democracy, women's rights, capitalism, and national priorities. They found that as countries industrialize, as people leave the land and enter factories, wealth rises and values shift. But there is also a downside. The increase in wealth makes people more materialistic and desirous of the social prestige that money buys. However, a few generations later these same economies transition to more service-based jobs that require a new set of skills and values compared to factory jobs. As economies get wealthier, the same societies also become safer and less vulnerable to natural disasters and political brutalization. Welzel explains that as existential pressures are reduced, people become more open, and they prioritize freedom, autonomy, diversity, and creativity. They start championing women's rights, animal rights, gay rights, human rights, poverty alleviation, and environmental preservation.[20] So we may speak of something that can be called a "gracious capitalism."

Some privately owned corporations, such as the Mars Foundation and Flow Automotive Companies in the United States, just to mention two, care for employees, love their communities, and offer a gracious gift to the world. Leap International, the business I (Clive) oversee, has a foundation that serves and upbuilds some of the poor in Asia. The motive is more than just social and environmental awareness. For Christians in business, the motive is gratitude to God and love of neighbor.[21] Corporate social responsibility is now a global movement. It is sometimes done for the wrong motives—window-dressing a corporate image—but it at least is being done. And some neighbors are loved through it. Even some publicly traded companies, such as ServiceMaster, have been able to withstand the withering demand of shareholders for maximum profit because of the integrity of their embodied values and purpose. This, too, comes from the Christian gospel and the kingdom of God, the very gospel that in part has inspired capitalism and entrepreneurial initiative.

We started this chapter with the question of whether work in a capitalist economy, and the use of money to bring profitability to a corporation and its owners, could in some way be a contribution to the kingdom of God, that new world God is bringing into this world, a world of human flourishing and shalom. This question is important, since most people in the church are spending the majority of their waking hours in the system. Craig Gay, commenting on the parable of the shrewd manager, which we will take up in the next chapter, concludes,

> We should continue to work within the market system—making friends of the "mammon of unrighteousness"—but not for the sake of the system *per se* and not in such a way as to become captivated by the endlessly acquisitive "spirit" of the system, but rather *subversively* and for the sake of ends that entirely transcend the system . . . for the sake of *fellowship*, knowing full well that such is all that will survive into the world to come.[22]

How?

Grace can curb the lust for money. Grace can enable us to live and work in situations that are even demonic, provided we are called by God to work there, and to do so wholeheartedly and for God. In a system that monetizes things and people, grace enables us not to evaluate people by their financial clout. Grace insists that the process of making money is as important as what we do with the money made. Grace enables us to build organizational cultures that energize people and prize them. Amazingly, our work in the industrial, information, service, and creative sectors can become for us "doing the Lord's work," as it was for the slaves and masters in the Colossian society centuries ago, for they were imbued with the vision to work "with sincerity of heart and reverence for the

Lord" (Col. 3:22). Thus, the insidious dualism discussed in the last chapter is substantially overcome. A remarkable paper by a Chinese economist, Zhao Xiao, compares market economies without the church—namely the Chinese system—and economies with the church—namely in North America. He was charged with finding out why capitalism thrived in the United States. His conclusion is challenging though overstated. But it is this: the church restrains greed.[23] But especially in the West, where Christianity is diminishing and capitalism has substantially lost its moral charter, we must face the question of whether capitalism will last.

Post Capitalism?

Capitalism, according to Paul Mason, an economics writer, is a learning organism that adapts constantly, and sometimes drastically. At critical turning points, especially when threatened, it morphs and mutates into patterns and structures barely recognizable to the generation that came before. And capitalism's most basic survival instinct is to drive technological change. If we consider not just info-tech but food production, birth control, global health, and the introduction of robotics and artificial intelligence in all areas of life, the past twenty-five years have probably seen the greatest upsurge in human capability ever. But despite its adaptability, capitalism is fragile. Mason says, "Capitalism as a complex, adaptive system has nevertheless reached the limits of its capacity to adapt."[24] The long-term prospects, he maintains, are bleak. According to the Organization for Economic Co-operation and Development, growth in the developed world will be "weak" for the next fifty years.[25] Inequality will rise by 40 percent. Even in developing countries, in the majority world, the current dynamism will be exhausted by 2060. We have already seen signs of this.

What started in 2008 as an economic crisis in the United States spread to Western Europe and then it became a global crisis. The

economic stress became a social crisis, leading to mass unrest. Rev-
olutions like the Arab Spring arose, and now there are civil wars in
the Middle East and military tension between superpowers. One
of the fundamental drivers of this crisis is capitalism's inability to
engage all members of society. According to Nick Srnicek and Alex
Williams, "There is a growing population of people that are situated outside formal, waged work, making do with minimal welfare
benefits, informal subsistence work, or by illegal means."[26] This
dark side of capitalism is highlighted in a short piece of fiction by
Jonathan Haidt:

> Once upon a time, work was real and authentic. Farmers raised
> crops and craftsmen made goods. People traded those goods lo-
> cally, and that trade strengthened local communities. But then,
> Capitalism was invented, and darkness spread across the land.
> The capitalists developed ingenious techniques for squeezing
> wealth out of workers, and then sucking up all of societies' re-
> sources for themselves. The capitalist class uses its wealth to
> buy political influence, and now the 1% is above the law. The
> rest of us are its pawns, forever. The end.[27]

Mason, mentioned earlier, warns that unless a new alternative to
capitalism is found, the present system of capitalism will degenerate into one of two likely scenarios. In the first, the global elite
clings on, imposing on workers, pensioners, and the poor the cost
of the crisis over the next ten or twenty years. The global order—as
enforced by the International Monetary Fund (IMF), World Bank,
and World Trade Organization—survives, but in a weakened form.
The cost of saving globalization is borne by ordinary people of the
developed world. But growth stagnates.

In the second scenario, the consensus breaks. Parties of the hard
right and left come to power as ordinary people refuse to pay the
price of austerity. Instead, states then try to impose the costs of the

crisis on each other. Globalization falls apart. Global institutions become powerless. The conflicts that have simmered during these past twenty years—drug wars, post-Soviet nationalism, jihadism, uncontrolled migration and resistance to it—light a fire at the center of the system. In this scenario, lip-service paid to international law evaporates. Torture, censorship, arbitrary detention, and mass surveillance become the regular tools of statecraft. This is a variant of what happened in the 1930s, and there is no guarantee it cannot happen again.

In both scenarios, the serious impacts of climate change, demographic aging, and population growth kick in around the year 2050. If we cannot create a sustainable global order and restore economic dynamism, the decades after 2050 will be chaotic. But there may be other options.

In response to these bleak outlooks, others have proposed various forms of socialism in which there is some degree of central economic planning with shared or public ownership of resources. Still others have called for more participation from workers and consumers operating through decision-making councils. Robin Hahnel argues for a participatory economy, in which economic benefits will be aligned with needs, the amount of which would be determined democratically by worker and consumer councils.[28] Hahnel believes "economic justice" is reachable when people are rewarded for their effort and diligence rather than accomplishments or prior ownership.

In the midst of these morbid scenarios, Jacques Ellul offers a reminder, though not a consoling one, that "our struggle is not against flesh and blood, but against . . . the powers of this dark world and against the spiritual forces of evil in the heavenly realms" (Eph. 6:12). So while there may never in this life be a perfect economic system, we will necessarily live in the present system with continuous tension. To do this well, Ellul argues for personal contemplation that will enable us to keep money in its proper place and to behave with consistency in relation to the handling of money, something we are attempting to do in this book.

> The course of history belongs to God, and if we as Christians have any influence on it, it is first of all by our faithfulness to his will. Everything that tends to turn us away from this faithfulness diminishes Christian effectiveness, even if outwardly we do a great deal, changing institutions and mobilizing the masses.[29]

It is this very issue of effectiveness in our handling of money to which we now turn as we examine the outrageous parable of Jesus, the parable of the shrewd manager.

6

How to Buy Forever Friendships

Until we reclaim the language of effectiveness and shrewdness we will continue to find ourselves outmaneuvered, much like the master was by the manager, by the forces of pride and greed which have so gripped the modern workplace.

Daniel Draht,
employment lawyer[1]

In the last chapter we explored the reality of capitalism, how it started, its extraordinary fruitfulness, and its problems. We considered whether we can participate in the capitalist system as a way of embracing the kingdom of God, as something that would be pleasing to God. In this book, we are exploring what it means to live a unified life, usually called an "integrated" life, where there is a no sacred-secular distinction. And we discovered that while Christianity is partly responsible for the rise of capitalism, the capitalist system is now generally bereft of its founding moral charter. And yet it is possible and even life-giving for us and others to participate in this system in a kingdom of God way. Indeed, even if we are working for a nonkingdom corporation or organization, we can still do that work in a God-honoring and neighbor-loving way. All good work is kingdom of God work.[2] So in the last chapter we quoted Craig Gay in his reflection on the parable of the shrewd manager in proposing that our work in the system is not for the system *per se* but for fellowship with God and our neighbors near and far. But now we must examine the parable in greater detail because it has such obvious relevance for our personal and effective use of money.

The story of the shrewd manager is a marketplace parable. In the gospels, Jesus seems to be almost always using stories from the work world, from the world of buying and selling, from the handling of money (bags of gold, for example), and from the normal occupations of people working in the world. He wants to tell us about the kingdom of God, that wonderful good news of a new world coming and now present in people's lives, as well as partially present in society. But he does this by teaching and ministering in the public square, not mainly in the synagogue or the temple. And in selecting followers, he called twelve normal working people, not rabbis and priests, and some of his chosen ones had questionable occupations. Why would he do this? One reason is that Jesus was immersed in the work world for twenty or thirty years as an entrepreneur carpenter, making tables and chairs, designing and building houses or boats. But there is another reason. Jesus was concerned with the integration of faith and life. To obtain this integration, he had to speak to and from the normal work and money-handling lives of ordinary people. Something similar happened to me (Paul).

Earlier I said that I (Paul) grew up in a business home. My father was the president of a steel fabrication company, and I worked in that business in every role except becoming president. Later, I worked in carpentry and in a renovation business. So it is not surprising that I ultimately became a professor of marketplace theology. Not surprisingly, many of the teachings of Jesus have a marketplace context—most of them in fact, especially the very strange parable of Jesus that is found in Luke 16:1–9.

Parables are not factual stories but conceived narratives, cameos, in which an image is cast into our consciousness that will send us reeling, send us on a journey of discovery, all to introduce us to the kingdom of God. This was Jesus's primary message—the good news of the kingdom of God, namely that God is bringing into this world and to people shalom, human flourishing, and new life. "Jesus went into Galilee, proclaiming the good news of God. 'The time has come,' he said. 'The kingdom of God has come near. Repent and believe the good news!'" (Mark 1:14–15). Not only will the coming kingdom save people's souls, but it will bring transformation to everything else, including what we do with money. And this parable is about money.

In his commentary on this parable N. T. Wright notes:

> About half the stories in the newspapers seem to be about money in one way or another—the glamour and the glitz it seems to provide, the shock and the horror when it runs out, the never-ending scandals about people getting it, embezzling it, losing it and getting it again. The lines between legitimate business and sharp practice are notoriously blurred. When does a gift become a bribe? When is it right to use other people's money to make money for yourself, and when is it wrong? And then there are robberies, burglaries, and the numerous other obvious ways in which money is at the centre of simple, old-fashioned wrongdoing.[3]

Is money good, bad, or neutral? In this parable, Jesus calls money "unrighteous mammon" or "worldly wealth," as it is sometimes translated. However, the word it translates in the original Greek communicates that money is stained; it has a bad potential; it can claim to be a god deserving our utter loyalty. Of course, it can also be used for good purposes. But one thing you cannot say about money—and this is what people want to say—is that money is neutral. It is spiritually radioactive. It gives a charge that can be used for good or ill. It is one of the powers which were created by God as good and for God. It has become polluted through sin, but it can be redeemed. And that is what this parable is about: being sent by Jesus into the world to use money in a transformative way, redemptively, as part of God's kingdom mission. In the last chapter, we explored gracious capitalism. Here we consider being gracious stewards of money as individuals. But first let us take in the story.

Don't Copy This Model

As is often the case, Jesus tells a story of a person that he does not want us to copy. This person is a scoundrel. But Jesus uses this contrived person to make a point that you cannot miss. There was an employee, whom we are calling the *manager*. But there was another important character. There was the *master* who owned a business. The manager was accused of wasting the master's money. It might have been hearsay, because the text has the master saying, "What is this I hear about you?" He had to give an account of his stewardship and was told he would be fired. Very bad news. But maybe the manager was not so bad.

Daniel Draht is a lawyer who specializes in employee terminations. He makes a fascinating observation about this parable, namely, that it is the master, not the manager, who is presented in a bad light.

> I can see no reasonable basis to conclude that a long-term, high-ranking employee who is terminated for dishonesty summarily by his employer would necessarily contest the decision in that instant. In fact, I see many psychological reasons why an effective defense on the spot is implausible in light of the inevitable emotional trauma the exchange must have inflicted upon the manager. Further justification for silence can be found in the fact that the charges the manager faced were profoundly vague. If the manager is innocent there is no way for him to know what the master is hearing about him. I also suggest that the text indicates an unwillingness of the master to listen to

the manager's defense. . . . In light of the above, I suggest the appropriate conclusion is that the master, not the servant, is actually portrayed negatively.[4]

The manager is about to be fired. But there is a pause between the accusation and the implementation of the firing. Again Draht, the employment lawyer, brings an interesting perspective:

> Instead of using fraud, I suggest the manager utilizes a technical ambiguity in his master's order to his advantage. . . . The manager utilized the ambiguity in his own favor, as is suggested by his thoughts after the meeting when he considers his future *after his removal from management has taken effect*, the implication being that it has not taken effect yet. . . . If the termination has not yet taken effect, the manager is entitled to continue with the responsibilities of manager until it does take effect.[5]

No question about it, being fired is hard. It is a devastating experience, especially when you are over fifty. And this manager is trying to figure out what he can do in this situation to sustain himself and his family. First, he says to himself, I am not strong enough to dig ditches. I (Paul) worked as a carpenter in Vancouver after being pastor of a large church. I remember pushing wheelbarrows full of drain rock on rickety scaffolding to dump them into the drainage trench around the house we were building. It was February, rain was pouring, and the temperature was just above freezing. But I was young, at least younger. Today when I look at what is involved in these high-energy trades, I say to myself, I cannot do it—like this poor manager in the story. There must be an alternative.

Then the manager thinks he could possibly beg for some money. But he is ashamed to do it.[6] He does not want to join the people at street corners who appeal to motorists for money while the stoplight is red. He will not put up a sign, wear shabby clothes, and hit on people. So, what to do? He thinks, "Ah, I know what I'll do so that when I lose my job people will look after me. They will welcome me into their homes." So here is where the parable gets really interesting.

He goes to his boss's creditors, people who owe his boss money, and does something smartly strategic, possibly controversial, certainly unexpected, and unquestionably enigmatic. Much ink has been spilled on what the manager actually was doing. Was he cutting his commission? Was he embezzling money from his boss? Was he writing down debt out of the principal that was loaned? Was he eliminating interest owed on the debt? On this last point, to really understand this story you need to know that Jews, following the Old Testament law, were forbidden to take interest from fellow Jews when they loaned money. It is called "usury" in the Bible, and throughout the history of the church it has been a big issue about which even great theologians like Luther and Calvin disagreed. Here is what seems to have occurred.

It appears that the master has loaned assets to his debtors and probably did this at a very high rate of interest, something he should not have done. Behind this is the possibility, which we are not told, that the clients to whom he loaned money and assets were also people of God—therefore, there should have been no interest involved.

So, the manager goes to the first debtor and says, "How much do you owe?" "Nine hundred gallons (or three thousand liters) of olive oil." That is a lot of cooking fat. "Well," says the manager, "let's make that fifteen hundred liters—exactly half" and gets the debtor to sign a document that this is all he now owes the master. In fact, the amount saved was what a single olive grove would produce in a whole year.[7] Is the story far-fetched?

In our developed economies where interest rates are kept low and are even going lower as governments try to encourage growth and control inflation, it is inconceivable that interest payments could account for half the debt. But maybe it is not far-fetched.

I (Clive) have an employee from Myanmar who was in a similar predicament as the debtor in the parable. This employee borrowed from the community leader in her village at 3.5 percent interest a month, or 42 percent annually. At this rate, her debt doubled every twenty months. She was unable to meet her interest payments and within a few years her debt grew several times the original loan amount. If she failed to pay her community leader, most likely her land would be confiscated, and she would eventually lose everything to pay down her debt. She and her family would still be indebted if the properties she sold could not cover the debt, and they would end up working in the farm of the community leader. Fortunately, like the shrewd manager, we were able to find a solution for her indebtedness. Unfortunately, however, such usury is still practiced in rural villages and communities throughout parts of Asia. The first debtor in Jesus's story has a lot of faces and names in the modern world. But there is a second one.

Then the manager goes to a second debtor and says, "How much do you owe?" "A thousand bushels of wheat," he says. That, once again, is a lot of wheat—thirty tons by some measurements. "Well, I have the power to change that amount to twenty-two tons, a 20 percent reduction." The debtors thought they had won the lottery! They loved the manager. *But they also loved the master.*

Doing the Best You Can in the Situation

In passing, it is useful to note that the manager made his master look great. In the process of making these deals, the manager endeared the master to the debtors, not only to himself. Indeed, any attempt to remove the manager would remove some of the goodwill that had accrued to the master.[8] It is a curious case of loving neighbor and self at the same time. Then comes the bombshell in the text.

"The master [the boss in the story] commended the dishonest manager because he had acted shrewdly." He must have said something like, "You got me! You worked smartly. You served me and yourself at the same time by your shrewd action." "For," Jesus goes on, "the people of this world are more shrewd in dealing with their own kind than are the people of the light" (Luke 16:8). This is a truthful and evocative observation. Secular people in business are often more cunning and shrewd in dealing with their own kind than are people of faith. Business depends on trust, and believers tend to be more trusting, more willing to give others the benefit of the doubt. Churches, Christian organizations, and individual Christians have often been scammed by cunning and sharp operators. I (Paul) have experienced this. Often, while trying to be trusting and compassionate, Christians are cunningly manipulated. They are often seen as "soft touches." And so, elsewhere, Jesus says, "Be as shrewd as snakes and as innocent as doves" (Matt. 10:16). This is surely one of the most significant things Jesus said for people involved in enterprises in the world. The combination is brilliant: innocence—being blameless and refusing to do wrong—combined with shrewdness—doing the thing that makes the maximum impact, working smart, investing wisely, and getting the biggest bang for the buck. Jesus exemplified it. He was without sin but was eminently strategic and unquestionably and positively shrewd.

The word in Greek for shrewd[9] or wise[10] is *phronimos*, referring to being intelligent, wise, or prudent, that is, mindful of one's interests and having a hard-headed acumen. But Jesus does not stop there; he goes on to insist that the disciples must at the same time be innocent[11] or harmless.[12] The Greek word for innocent or harmless, *akeraios*, is also understood to mean pure of heart, free from guile, innocent, and harmless. It is instructive to note that our shrewd acumen to look after our own interest must be harmless to the people we live with or work with. Beautifully in Matthew 10:16, Jesus reminds us to be shrewd in our heads but compassionate and pure in our hearts. Jesus seems to imply that only with this combination can we advance the kingdom.

Further, far from condemning shrewdness as wrong, though it can be, Jesus intimates and affirms a holy shrewdness. Take initiative in a smart way. But don't take advantage of others. Don't wait around for the perfect situation. Act now and strategically.

To be shrewd you must calculate the most effective way of moving forward. Draht, noting that Luke 16 follows the parable of the prodigal son in Luke 15 (which emphasizes forgiveness), comments how the modern Western church has concentrated on compassion and missed the *effectiveness* promoted in Luke 16:

> I am . . . suggesting that the type of effectiveness raised in the parable of the unrighteous steward is of a kind that is distinct from the type of effectiveness that grips our culture. The former [effectiveness portrayed in the parable] emphasizes effectiveness in creating benefits that flow to self, the latter [effectiveness in our culture] emphasizes benefits that flow to God's kingdom.[13]

Now, having told the story, Jesus speaks directly. This is not part of the parable but is based on it. "I tell you, use worldly wealth to gain friends for yourselves, so that when it is gone, you will be welcomed into eternal dwellings" (v. 9). The parable is understandably controversial and rarely preached in church sermons. Some regard it as the most challenging parable in the four Gospel accounts of Jesus.[14] When we hear Jesus say, "Use money to make friends for yourselves," we gasp. "Really?" And when the money fails, Jesus continues, when you die—and no armored money truck will follow the hearse—it is your friends who will welcome you into the eternal homes. What can this possibly mean?

The Enigma of a Commercial Friendship

It certainly does not mean we are to use money to buy friendship, which is the commercialization of relationships. Friendship is not

for anything except for the relationship itself. It may start with sharing a common interest; it may progress to where you care for another's identity, their well-being, their interests, and their passions.
It may develop to become an intimate friendship in which you share
your heart and soul. In such a relationship, you can name the lie in
another and encourage the development of their talents and gifts.
Friendship is clearly for mutual benefit, as was the case in the parable, but it is not something you can buy. We can, however, use money
in a way that creates and builds friendships. Needless to say, we find
some ambiguity about the true meaning of this word from Jesus.

In order fully to understand this fascinating text, we have to put
the story into the context of the whole chapter. Chapter 16 is like
a fish sandwich with two slices of bread and canned salmon in the
middle. One slice, the bread on top, is this story of a manager who
used money to gain friends who would last and care for him. The
second slice of bread, the slice on the bottom, is verses 19–31, the
story of a poor man named Lazarus and a rich man. The contrast
is arresting. The rich man was dressed in purple and fine linen. He
lived in luxury "every day" (v. 19). He lived in a mansion with a gate.
At the gate was Lazarus, the poor man. Lazarus "was laid" at the
gate by others. He was powerless even to get to his favorite begging
spot. He longed to pick up the scraps from the rich man's table.
Besides being destitute he was unwell. The final pitiable detail was
this: "Even the dogs came and licked his sores." He was a fixture in
the estate, not unlike the contrast of my (Paul's) family home in
Ontario with the Jupp shack next door.

But who was listening to Jesus tell this story of the rich man and
the poor man at the gate?

Jesus was telling these stories in the presence of the Pharisees,
who loved money and treated Jesus the way the rich man treated
Lazarus. Why did they act this way? Because Jesus had associated
himself with the poor, the blind, the outcast, the lepers, and the
sinful. Jesus was the man at the gate.

Then something happened, something cataclysmic. Both men died. The poor man, Lazarus, went to Jewish heaven, the bosom of Abraham. We are not told why he went to heaven. Did he, as a poor person, depend on God, for Luke's Gospel shows repeatedly how the poor are dependent on God, in contrast to the rich who are independent, self-satisfied, and have no need of God?[15] The rich man, in contrast, went to Jewish hell. There in agony he sees Lazarus and wants Lazarus to go back to the living and warn his five rich brothers. But Lazarus cannot do this because there is a gulf fixed between them. Then comes a bombshell. N. T. Wright says it is like the final crashing chord of a massive pipe organ.[16] Jesus says enigmatically that, even if someone comes back from the dead, referring to his own future resurrection, people will not believe unless they listen to Moses and prophets. Amazingly, Jesus takes the death warrant on his own life and turns it into a teaching moment. He is saying that even though he will be resurrected from the grave after he is crucified, people will not believe in him because of his resurrection unless they are willing to respond to the Word of God already expressed through Moses (the first five books of the Bible) and the prophets. And what do Moses and the prophets say?

Loving Our Neighbors Financially

They say to undertake justice and to show mercy. The law and the prophets are summarized in the New Testament by Jesus: to love God with all your heart, soul, strength, and mind and to love your neighbor as yourself (Matt. 22:37–39). To use what you possess to care for others. The manager, scoundrel that he was, loved his neighbor and himself at the same time!

And right there in the middle of the salmon sandwich, where the filling is, Jesus says the law and the prophets were proclaimed until the time of John the Baptist. Now people are forcing their way into the kingdom of God, desperately wanting with all their hearts

God's new world that is coming (Luke 16:16–17). And what do we learn from the law and the prophets? In the words of Jesus: I was hungry and you fed me, lonely and you visited me, naked and you clothed me—you showed caring, gratuitous love. To use what we have to care for others.

There it is. Jesus is not saying, use money to buy friendship. He is saying, use it to care for others. This is what it means to be sent into the work of the kingdom of God. And some of the relationships that emerge as we care for others will outlast this life. You are not actually buying eternal friendship and certainly not buying salvation. Rather, you are loving your neighbor. But one by-product of this will be more-than-this-life relationships. This is the very thing that the rich man in the parable refused to do.

You can do this in a million different ways: direct support, a meal brought to a home, a visit to someone who is lonely, a meal out with someone, direct assistance with no strings attached, supporting Christian and so-called secular agencies that are helping refugees, using money to take a trip to visit a friend in need, paying off the debt someone has who cannot do it themselves, and providing medical service in very dangerous places. This all needs to be done with love and shrewdness by being a smart investor. The parable assumes that there is no long-term security in one's job in this life, even with skills, integrity, and shrewdness. But if you love money, as the Pharisees do, you will not want to part with it but will want more and more. Jesus gets at the root of the result of loving money when he says you cannot serve two masters, God and money.

And the return for this investment? In terms of working in the world, you can invest in a business, work in a corporation, and participate in the capitalist system with grace and, as an amazing result, build relationships that can outlast this world. And individually, as you shrewdly use money, there can be a more-than-this-life result. Probably the result with not be increased material wealth. But you will have made some relationships in the forever family of

God that will last beyond the grave. And on the other side, when we wake up in the new heaven and new earth, there will be some people there who say, "Come on in. Welcome! You can stay with us in the grandest reunion in all eternity and the greatest home and homeland for humankind."

7

Why Money "Talks"—
the Social Value of Money

We should be asking when, how, and which forms of
money threaten social well-being but also: when does
money enhance moral concerns and sustain social
lives? Under what conditions does monetization ad-
vance justice and equality?

Viviana Zelizer,
The Social Meaning of Money[1]

When we say, "money talks," we are implying that money has
meaning. In fact, the use of money is like the use of language,
which carries gestures and symbols in our daily lives. "Like language, monetary symbols must be visible and interpretable by the
relevant audiences if they are to convey their meaning effectively,"
says sociologist George Herbert Mead.[2] But monetary symbols are
based on social conventions rather than just impersonal economic
transactions. So like language, money communicates meaning but,
unlike language, money only facilitates economic exchange while
language does many more things.[3] That being said, as a means of
communicating value and meaning money can also have a negative
effect, even on a whole society.

The Bad and Good Influence of Money on Society

In *The Philosophy of Money*,[4] perhaps Georg Simmel's most important work, he expounds the ways in which money has transformed
human interactions by making it possible for us to be impersonal.
Simmel argues that the economy is about interactions focused on
exchange rather than relationships of production, thus providing a
distinctive alternative to Marxian understandings. Yet at the same
time, Simmel agrees with Marx that contemporary life is character-
ized by something like alienation. He notes that money makes our
interactions more instrumental and calculable in character, and
that acquiring money can become an end in itself. The result has
been a subtle transformation of human society. Individuality and
care are removed from interactions, to be replaced by hardness,
a matter-of-fact attitude, and a "calculative exactness of practical
life."[5] The historian Fernand Braudel reflects that "any society based
on an ancient structure which opens its doors to money sooner or
later loses its acquired equilibria and liberates forces that can never
afterwards be adequately controlled."[6] This is what happened in the
medieval society of the West.

As the medieval economy became increasingly monetarized,
historians note, a causal connection arose between money's spread
and undesirable social change.[7] This led to the situation that Karl
Marx elaborated. Throughout the seventeenth and eighteenth
centuries, money had been the locus for deep-seated anxieties
about social instability and a powerful symbol of whatever ailed
society. Karl Marx therefore critiqued capitalism and was con-
vinced that the cash-nexus,[8] the depersonalized cash relationship
between employers and employees in a capitalist society, would
lead to a massive reduction in social values. Instead of authentic
pre-existing social relations, our social interactions would become
anonymous economic transactions.[9] But that is not the only thing

that money does in social relationships. While in theory money is impersonal, quantifiable, logical, and instrumental, in practice it is very different.

In practice, people attempt to personalize money and create labels and restrictions. Sociologist Bruce Carruthers argues that "money-in-practice is fraught with internal distinctions, and is carefully separated from sacred objects and certain social relations."[10] So it is the practice of using money based on social conventions that creates meaning for people. And these differentiations in the use of money are recognized socially rather than individually. This becomes apparent when we look at the "market."

Distinguished social scientist and prize-winning author Viviana Zelizer is among a group that challenged the neoclassical model of a single, autonomous, self-sustaining market. Instead, these sociologists view the market as a model of social or kinship networks shaped by ongoing changes in the buyers' and sellers' relationships in increasingly diverse cultural contexts. This alternative view of the market allows us to focus on small-scale counterparts of large-scale processes to study the integral parts of the process of spending and saving by consumers. So economic sociology is moving away from exclusive attention to businesses and capitalist markets to study households, markets for human goods, art, care work, and informal economies, taking account of gender, race, and other social differentiations. These studies enable sociologists to develop a better understanding of how we align money with our social interactions and context, in a word, our values. Values are simply cherished ways of behaving.

Earmarking Money for Social Values

One of Zelizer's key ideas is that monetary meaning is created by the "earmarking" of money. Through this people create qualitative differences in what is otherwise homogenous money. In the nineteenth century, for example, people made love tokens for loved ones to wear from gold coins. People also segregate monies spatially, using different domestic containers like envelopes, jars, or stockings to separate it. Earmarking takes place when money is used for different purposes, such as a wife's income for the children while a husband's pay for the mortgage. Further earmarking takes place when we create different systems of allocation: household income, money for gifts, or cash available for emergencies—all based on domestic principles. This is clearly a social process where different sums of money are tagged to reinforce a social structure.

Instead of treating money as an impersonal instrument, people deliberately "identify, classify, organize, use, segregate, manufacture, design, store, and even decorate monies" to cope with and to bring meaning to their multiple social relations, as Zelizer notes.[11] For example, a study of the Oslo prostitution trade in the 1980s found that money earned from prostitution was squandered on "going out" and on drugs, alcohol, and clothes. These monies "burnt a hole in the pocket" and were spent quickly. On the other hand, welfare money, health benefits, or other legal incomes made by these same people were carefully budgeted and spent for the "straight life," to pay rent and bills.[12] They would sweat laboriously to ensure that legal money was well used for the "straight part" of their lives. Another study in Philadelphia in the 1950s that focused on a gang member by the name of Marty found clear demarcation about his sources and usages of money. He mentioned how he donated to the church the twenty-five cents given to him by his mother. On the other hand, money generated from his gang activities could not be given to the church. "Oh no, that is bad money, that is not honest money."[13] In both these examples, the use of money was guided by feelings of shame, security, approval, and love—subjective controls rather than objective and impersonal considerations.

I (Clive) also have a system of earmarking my sources of income. I generate income from working in business and also from teaching and speaking in theological schools and churches. Different sources are matched with different targets. I budget my income from business and use it for family and personal expenses. I keep my receipts from teaching and speaking in a separate envelope (if received in cash) or in a special bank account and use them strictly for giving to mission or buying theological and spiritual books. I never thought about it in the beginning, but I was and am creating distinctions in my sources of income. I don't think this is a duality of secular and sacred but a need to create meanings from a collection of seemingly homogenous monies.

Behind this idea of earmarking is the belief that not all money is equal or exchangeable. The distinctiveness lies in identifying the sources of the money and matching it with its target uses, again relating to values. So Zelizer offers a refreshing alternative view of money that can inform us about our human relationships and failings. For too long, money has been viewed with deep suspicion as corrupting and dehumanizing. As Zelizer argues, "We should be asking when, how, and which forms of money threaten social well-being but also: when does money enhance moral concerns and sustain social lives? Under what conditions does monetization advance justice and equality?"[14] This distinction between various values for money also applies to the sacred and profane meanings of money.

Sacred versus Profane

Russell Belk and Melanie Wallendorf, distinguished research professors, argue that our need to differentiate between sources and uses of money lies in our interpretation of the boundaries between the sacred and the profane. According to Belk and Wallendorf, in our consumer society, money is an invisible but omnipresent god—revered, feared, worshipped, and treated with the highest respect.[15] Money is not neutral. "As an object with sacred power, money can be either good (e.g., religious donations, the 'nest egg') or evil (e.g., blood money, ransom money)."[16] The ability of the sacred to be simultaneously expressed as an "either beneficent or evil power produces, in the reverent [person], ambivalent feelings of fascination and repulsion termed kratophany."[17]

That which is sacred is extraordinary and invokes strong feelings within individuals in a community. To spend money on education, rent, and food is sacred because of the high regard with which we hold our families and their well-being. The funds for these sacred areas are sourced from wholesome and legitimate sources. On the other hand, the funds from illegitimate sources are used for consuming alcohol, smoking cigarettes, and gambling—activities we consider profane. There is a fear that illegitimate, "dirty" sources of funds will somehow contaminate the sacred realms of our lives. Belk and Wallendorf conclude in their survey on the sacred meaning of money:

> Prior treatments of money have concentrated almost entirely on its profane meanings. This utilitarian view encourages the fiction that contemporary market transactions are impersonal and without deeper sacred meanings. We are just beginning to realize the extent to which the modern market is still imbedded in personal and social meanings. . . . While the co-present good and evil sides of sacred money entail certain risks, we believe this risk is justified in light of the alternative of a purely profane society.[18]

The book of Judges carries an important example of mixing the profane and the sacred resulting in the long and painful consequences of idolatry. Micah, a man from the hill country of Ephraim, returned eleven hundred shekels he had stolen from his mother. In gratitude, Micah's mother pledged two hundred shekels to be turned into an idol by a silversmith. A profane act of thievery was turned into a "sacred" idol and kept in Micah's house. "Now this man Micah had a shrine, and he made an ephod and some idols and installed one of his sons as his priest. In those days Israel had no king; everyone did as he saw fit" (Judg. 17:5–6). The six hundred Danites that came and annihilated the city of Laish coveted the idol and took it with them, with dire spiritual consequences. "They continued to use the idols Micah had made, all the time the house of God was in Shiloh" (Judg. 18:31).

Another example of mixing profane and sacred is found in the New Testament book of Matthew. Judas threw the thirty silver coins he was paid for betraying Jesus into the temple. Then he left and hanged himself. Even the vindictive and merciless chief priests, who were indifferent to the plight of their accomplice (Matt. 27:4), were careful in handling the coins. "It is against the law to put this into the treasury, since it is blood money," they said. So, they decided to use the money to buy the potter's field as a burial place for foreigners (vv. 6–7). The example of Judas Iscariot is an extreme one in which only one thing is sacred and everything else is profane, a confusion of boundaries. Judas's single devotion to money desecrated all other areas of his life and relationships. He was the treasurer of the disciple group, probably volunteering for the job, but was reported by John to have helped himself to the collection (John 12:6). He betrayed the trust of the disciples. He pretended to want to sell an expensive perfume to give to the poor (John 12:4–5) but actually regretted seeing a year's wages going to anoint Jesus's feet instead of into his own pocket. Perhaps he could not believe in Jesus because he already had a "god." What kind of a person would betray for thirty silver coins a friend with whom he had lived and worked for three years? There was only one thing in Judas's life that was sacred—money. There was no room for another. By money he lived; by money he died. But sacred and profane distinctions are not the only distinctions we make in the value expressed in our use of money.

Money and Gender

In an interview with author Liz Perle, Stephen Goldbart, a psycho-
therapist who co-founded the Money, Meaning, and Choices Institute, observes that historically, men and women have different roles
regarding money. The role of men as providers has not changed in
thousands of years, and masculine identity and power came from
this age-old survival-based model.[19] According to Goldbart, today
men are still defined first by their work and financial success and
second by their family.[20] Our societies look up to men who have the
potential to provide generously. Lack of money brings shame to a
man, because it reflects his inability to provide. The pressure is high.
Money-talk is a man's talk. It remains largely unchanged despite
the increasing contribution women are making to family finances.
While the feminist movement has reshaped the relationship between women and money, for men it remains largely untouched.
Men think (not unjustly) that women evaluate them by how much
wealth they can create and how much money they can provide.
Women won't admit it, but they do, says Liz Perle.

In another interview, Pamela York Klainer, a financial entrepreneur and author of *How Much Is Enough?*, observes that men
use money as a differentiator between themselves and other men
and associate money with power. Men use money to buy expensive
gifts for the people around them to show that they "have arrived."
Women, on the other hand, use money to express their love and
to nurture bonds and relationships.[21] Floyd Rudmin proposes that
"women do not think of money as power as frequently as do men;
instead, women think of money in terms of the things into which
it can be converted, while men think of it in terms of the power its
possession implies."[22] An earlier study found that even the money
earned by women from selling eggs and housing boarders was considered trivial, despite the crucial fact that it supplemented meeting
the needs of the household.[23]

Two Harvard professors lament that businesses do not recognize the economic power of women. According to the authors, "Women make the decision in the purchases of 94% of home furnishings ... 92% of vacations ... 91% of homes ... 60% of automobiles ... [and] 51% of consumer electronics."[24] They may or may not be the key income earners at home, but they certainly are the key decision makers on how the income is to be spent. The Bible gives an example of this dichotomy between the main decision-maker and the main earner in the household of the "surly and mean" Nabal (1 Sam. 25:3). When David sent ten young men to offer greetings and make a request for food, Nabal went into a power struggle with David: "Why should I take my bread and water, and the meat I have slaughtered for my shearers, and give it to men coming from who knows where?" (v. 11). Though he was a wicked man and "no one can talk to him" (v. 17), his wife Abigail was in control of the food and "took two hundred loaves of bread, two skins of wine, five dressed sheep, five seahs of roasted grain, a hundred cakes of raisins and two hundred cakes of pressed figs, and loaded them on donkeys" (v. 18) and so appeased David. The male thinks he is in charge, but it is the woman who makes the decision for the household—so it has traditionally gone. But there is more to the gender differentiation than power.

In *Money as Sacrament*, Adele Azar-Rucquoi examines the central role money plays for women in their outlook on life, relationships, confidence, independence, and inner peace.[25] Azar-Rucquoi grew up running the cash register at her immigrant father's grocery. She despised her father's obsession with money and rebelled by being a nun for several years. She eventually became the wife of a formerly homeless man, and, ironically, was the unexpected heir, later in life, to a substantial inheritance left by her astute father. Shaped by her own struggles with money, she encourages women to recognize the important role of money in their lives and to recognize its inherently multifaceted meaning.

For some women, their relationship with money is more complex. Liz Perle, writing in her memoir, went so far as to admit that "money [as] an aphrodisiac may rank among the most politically incorrect confessions a woman can make—but that doesn't make it any less real." She confesses that money is important yet admits that this is superficial and materialistic. She says that while it is taboo to discuss money in public, it is central to many private conversations. "We may condemn our wants as crass consumerism, yet we can be stopped dead in our tracks at the thought of losing our lifestyles."[26] But there is another dimension of the relational value of money.

Money and Love

Money plays a significant role with a woman and a man in love or in a marriage. Through the giving and sharing of money, a person perceives whether he or she is esteemed. It can become a tool that communicates how a couple feels about one another. It can be a symbol for love. For example, one wise woman, Jean Chatzky, commented:

> I see a difference in older women and younger women. . . . A fifty-year-old absolutely sees money as a means to an end. And a twenty-five-year-old hasn't gotten there yet. Older women have [a] deeper understanding of what [it] can and can't do for them. Younger women tend to believe that money has the ability—if not to buy their happiness—then at least to buy the things that make them happy. Older women know that's not true.[27]

One surprising finding from recent surveys is the important role of credit score in courtship. The parent company of a leading dating site, the Match Media Group, in a survey of two thousand online daters, found financial responsibility as the leading quality in a potential mate. It came in at sixty-nine percent, ahead of sense of humor (67 percent), attractiveness (51 percent), ambition (50 percent), courage (42 percent), and modesty (39 percent). The survey found that a good credit score was associated with being responsible, trustworthy, and smart.[28]

Biological anthropologist Helen Fisher, Match.com's chief scientific adviser and a senior research fellow at the Kinsey Institute, calls credit score a "Darwinian mechanism for measuring your reproductive ability." She says, "If you've got a pretty good credit score, you probably have other good personality traits. . . . You're not only managing your money, you're managing your family, your friends. You're kind of a managing person. It says a lot more about you than a fancy car." She even called it "an honest indicator of who you really are."[29] Researchers from Texas A&M University and the University of Texas at Dallas concluded a similar thing in a 2015 study: "Credit scores matter for committed relationships because they reveal information about general trustworthiness."[30]

Even divorce rates can be predicted from credit scores, according to a 2015 study of roughly 12 million consumers by researchers at the Federal Reserve Board, the Brookings Institution, and UCLA. Those with higher credit scores are less likely to split from their partner, and vice versa. "Couples with the lowest initial average scores are two or three times more likely to separate than the couples with the highest average scores, and the likelihood of separation largely diminishes as scores increase," the study found.[31]

In a dating relationship, asking for one's credit score appears shallow and inappropriate, and some commentators observed that daters seem more willing to share about their sexual diseases than their financial histories. But sociologist Viviana Zelizer argues that for a relationship to work there must be a "good match" between economic activity and intimacy. "By good matches . . . I mean that the match is viable: it gets the economic work of the relationship done and sustains the relationship."[32] A Credit Scores and Committed Relationships paper found in 2015 that dating someone with a similar credit score increases the success of the relationship because married couples' credit scores tend to converge over time.[33] But all of this assumes that people are talking about money, and there are cultural differences in being willing to do so.

Eastern and Western Cultural Values

Before moving to North America, I, Clive, was told that it is impolite to talk about money in North America. I found out that this is true not only in society but in the church, as well. David Krueger calls it the last taboo.[34] "Whereas sex and death have been removed from both the social and the research taboo list in many Western countries, money is still a topic that appears to be impolite to discuss and debate."[35]

Liz Perle complained, "I know more about my friends' sexual assets than their financial ones. They've never hesitated to tell me all about love affairs, dreams, disappointments—even their husbands' most minute physical, moral, mental, and sexual failings—but I have no idea what any of them earn or spend each month."[36]

This reticence about money surprises me, because I come from Singapore, where money is discussed openly and freely. Friends who admire your new car will quickly ask how much you paid for it. Guests to your home will ask you about the cost of your furnishings. Gordon Redding, a European academic who lived in Hong Kong, observed that Westerners in Hong Kong and Singapore are frequently bemused to find Chinese people so ingenuous over the topic of money. He writes, "To be asked at a cocktail party how much you paid for your suit or what you are paying the caterers is for them perfectly normal and not something to be whispered out of earshot."[37] According to Redding, this frankness suggests that money itself is an especially potent symbol from which Chinese people derive important meanings. This might be attributed to the need for developing a psychological armory to fight the long battles of uncertainty and insecurity that were part of their history.

Chinese children are raised at an early age to value money, to bargain, and to save. This propensity to save is especially prevalent in those who grow up poor. It is not surprising that the gross saving rates in China and Singapore at forty-six and forty-eight percent, respectively, are among the highest in the world. Children of Chinese descent are brought up surrounded by anxieties and pragmatism about money, whereas in the West, possibly with fewer anxieties about the precariousness of life, people tend to be moralistic and negative when money is discussed. Education for many in Singapore is more about getting a good job and good pay rather than a means of expressing and actualizing oneself. Although this is changing rapidly as parts of Asia develop economically, anxiety about money continues to predominate from one generation to another. So, the East takes a pragmatic approach to money.

The reasons for Chinese pragmatism are four-fold. First, Chinese perception is immediate and sense-based, probably as a result of their use of Chinese logograms in writing, a system based on the senses and what can be seen. Second, under the ethical influence of Confucianism, Chinese morality is contingent rather than being based on absolutes. Third, social control comes principally from one's immediate circle. And fourth, dedication to family survival is a dominating motive for behavior. "In these circumstances the taking of decisions on what appear as practical grounds is to be expected,"[38] concludes Redding.

The fourth aspect of Chinese pragmatism is frugality. Chinese frugality "is more about self-denial (perhaps strictures within the family) than of an unashamed parsimony. It would be, for instance, almost inconceivable for a Chinese to emulate J. Paul Getty in providing guests with a pay phone."[39] The classic Chinese text *Dao De Jing* states that the three greatest treasures one can have are love, frugality, and generosity. Frugality, considered a virtue in Chinese culture, is taught to children at a very young age. An entrepreneur in Singapore notes:

> This is a realistic society. . . . If you do not have some status, some savings of your own, some success to back you up, it is of no use no matter how capable you are. . . . Therefore, one must realize the value of money and guard it well—not waste it so easily, it is the only vehicle that allows you to succeed eventually.[40]

We have been exploring how money is a social system, how it communicates social values, and how its acceptance is based on the meanings prescribed by a community. But can that happen with cryptocurrency?

Social Values and Cryptocurrency

In the last decades, significant advances in technologies enable many different payment systems such as PayPal, Apple Pay, and Ali Pay. These have become a daily part of our lives. When it comes to monetary media, the choices are varied: cash, plastic, and digital. But now there are more than a thousand types of cryptocurrencies with ever more organizations and even associations offering their own versions. It is not only technologies that will grow monetary plurality but also the growing influence of the millennial generation and their appreciation of technology. They bring a unique perspective to money.

Libra, the expected new cryptocurrency being developed by the social media giant Facebook, will have significant impact simply because Facebook has more than two billion community members. The use of different monetary media is as old as the history of money, and these media include shells, metal rods, silver, gold, sticks, and cigarettes. The important commonality with all these is the acceptance of that monetary medium as money within the community. Facebook has agreed to work within the official financial system unlike other currencies, like Bitcoins, that pride themselves on their anonymity. It is too early to know whether cryptocurrencies will achieve full acceptance like other monetary media without the sanction and support of the world's central banks.

We have been exploring the social value of money, how it has meanings in different contexts, how it expresses cherished ways of behaving, values, that relate to communities and even to genders. We return to Viviana A. Zelizer's question with which we began: "When does money enhance moral concerns and sustain social lives? Under what conditions does monetization advance justice and equality?" That raises the larger question of stewardship; that is, how we are to undertake the use of money in ways that conform to the purpose of God, the up-building of the community, and the flourishing of humankind?

8

Whose Money Is It Anyway?

"The silver is mine and the gold is mine," declares the LORD Almighty.

Haggai 2:8

The Jews were constrained to a regular payment of tithes; Christians, who have liberty, assign all their possessions to the Lord, bestowing freely not the lesser portions of their property, since they have hope of greater things.

Irenaeus[1]

In church circles, the word *stewardship* is commonly used to camouflage an appeal for funds for church and religious purposes. But in fact, the term denotes a more comprehensive view of life affecting time, work, leisure, talents, the state of one's soul, care for the environment, and, of course, money. The Greek word for *steward* (*oikonomos,* from which we get our word *economy*) means "one who manages a household." Years ago, persons called *stewards* were employed, rather than huge financial institutions, to manage the financial affairs and households of wealthy people. Their management included not only money but everything that makes a household thrive, not unlike the vocation of homemaking, but on a larger scale. A biblical example is Joseph's work as steward of Potiphar's house;

his master did not "concern himself with anything in the house" (Gen. 39:8).[2] In this chapter, we are considering personal and church stewardship, with a special focus on money. But stewardship starts with a transformative truth.

Managing God's Household

God is the ultimate owner of everything. "The earth is the LORD's, and everything in it, the world and all who live in it" (Pss. 24:1; 50:10). God has entrusted the nonhuman creation to the care of humankind. A good word to describe our double relationship with God and the world is *trusteeship*: we are entrusted with the care of the world and are accountable to God, who owns it and has declared his intended purpose for it. This trusteeship stems from the so-called creation mandate in Genesis 1:26–29. This all-encompassing stewardship is the calling of every human being. In the Old Testament, God (the divine owner) gives, as Chris Wright notes, "accredited discretionary power" to all humankind (Gen. 1:26–29) for the benefit of everyone.[3] But the people of God, Israel under the Old Testament and the church under the New, were given not only the calling valid for all humanity but some special responsibilities.

Under this first covenant, God's gift of trusteeship was especially directed to the nation Israel (Deut. 10:14–15). Families (more like clans or extended families today) provided the basic social, kinship, legal, and religious structures under the old covenant. They were family-plus-land units, as is graphically illustrated by the redemption of Naomi's land-plus-family in Bethlehem (Ruth 4:9–12). Thus, in the Jubilee year (which occurs every fifty years), both God's ultimate ownership and the family's trusteeship were expressed by the return of the land to the original family, even if the land had been mortgaged or sold in the meantime to pay debts (Lev. 25:4–18). The reason given is this: "The land is mine and you reside in my land as foreigners and strangers" (Lev. 25:23). This has implications for the question of providing an inheritance for one's own family.

Applying Old Testament legislation to people living under the gospel of the New Testament must be undertaken in a paradigmatic way—with the Old providing a structure for thinking about something greater that is fulfilled in the New. All the promises of God concerning God's presence, people, and place find their "yes" in Christ (2 Cor. 1:20). The gentiles along with Jews in Christ become joint heirs (Eph. 3:6) in a corporate body so that "in Christ" answers to all that "in the land" meant to Israel—and even more! Fellowship in Christ for the gentiles, as well as the Jews, fulfills the analogous function for the Christian as the possession of the land did for the Israelite. But that does not eliminate the socioeconomic dimension of stewardship. Christian fellowship (*koinōnia*) is not merely spiritual communion. It is total sharing of life, regarding possessions as not just one's own, and bringing economic peacemaking and social justice. We explored this in part in chapter six with the parable of the shrewd manager.

Christians share stewardship of the world with the rest of humankind, but we have three additional concerns: (1) the investment and proper use of our personal time, abilities, and finances for the benefit of others, something for which we are held responsible by God (Matt. 25:14–30); (2) the treasuring and distribution of the grace of God as proclaimed in the gospel (1 Pet. 4:10), not only by apostles and church leaders (1 Cor. 4:1; Titus 1:7) but by all believers being stewards and witnesses of the gospel; and (3) the full-fledged sharing of life (including material possessions) as a sign of being "in Christ." In the early church, this meant sharing available assets over and above the normal (Acts 2:44–45; 4:32–35), engaging in relief missions to poor believers (Acts 11:27–30), and cross-cultural giving to symbolize their mutual interdependence, equality, and unity in Christ (1 Cor. 16:1; 2 Cor. 8:13). But what about our stewardship of money?

Contrary to the secular viewpoint—"If you don't own it, you won't take care of it"—being a steward should increase our care and diligence in the use of property and wealth. It is not ours. It will be taken back by God one day. God will hold us responsible for what we do with it. And God wants not just an intact creation but a return on his investment.

It is tragic that Christian stewardship has been so often reduced to tithing—giving to the Lord's work one-tenth of one's income ("Is that gross or net after taxes?"). In the Old Testament, tithes were like taxes paid to the temple; they were not discretionary gifts (for an exception, see Gen. 14:20). This giving accomplished four things. It (1) celebrated the goodness of God (Deut. 14:26), (2) acknowledged God's ownership of everything, (3) maintained places of worship (Num. 18:21; Deut. 14:27), and (4) cared for the poor (Deut. 14:28–29). Even in the Old Testament, tithing was only part of Israel's stewardship. The New Testament only once mentions tithing (Matt. 23:23)—in the context of Jesus's calling the Pharisees to something more important. The New Testament principle is not one-tenth but "cheerful" giving, literally hilarious giving (2 Cor. 9:7), that is, uncalculating giving. R. T. France describes it as "an almost reckless generosity, motivated not by a sour sense of obligation but by a warm and unselfish compassion."[4] Since everything belongs to God, we should generously disburse what we can to help others. But the use of "should" destroys the very idea of Christian giving; it comes not from law or obligation but from the spontaneous overflow of gratitude for Christ's blessing on our lives (2 Cor. 8:9).

The Grace of Giving

Many people give donations. Donations imply that we own what we give and out of the generosity of our hearts we are giving some to others. Stewardship implies that it all belongs to God and is to be used for God's purposes. Donation spirituality is self-affirming and calculated for effect; stewardship spirituality is other-directed and wholehearted. Donation spirituality looks for a "Thank-you" from the recipient; stewardship spirituality aims at "Well done" when the Lord returns.

Some questions to ponder are these: How much do we give that does not come from a sense of obligation or social expectation? Do we act as if the part we retain is actually ours? Do we regard whatever wealth we have as a stewardship on behalf of the poor, as John Chrysostom proposed?[5] Does the disbursement of monies represented by our checkbook or credit card invoice reflect God's priorities for everyday life?

How does the grace of giving work out in practice? Of course, Christians should give to support Christian workers and causes, as we are instructed in Scripture. But in accordance with the Old Testament outlook, we should also see that we are stewards of money and assets in ways that benefit our families. To neglect family through sacrificing for the church is wrong. This is clearly something both Jesus (Mark 7:11) and Paul affirmed. Indeed, not taking care of our families makes us worse than unbelievers (1 Tim. 5:8). We should also heed Jesus's injunction to "use worldly wealth to gain friends for yourselves, so that when it is gone, you will be welcomed into eternal dwellings" (Luke 16:9). This means investing in people, giving money (anonymously, if possible) to the poor, and showing hospitality. As Thomas Aquinas so beautifully explained, this holistic stewardship is much more than handouts. He listed seven corporal (bodily) almsdeeds—to give drink to the thirsty, to feed the hungry, to clothe the naked, to harbor the harborless, to visit the sick, to ransom the captive, and to bury the dead. He linked them with seven spiritual almsdeeds—to instruct the ignorant, to counsel the doubtful, to comfort the sorrowful, to reprove the sinner, to forgive injuries, to bear with those who trouble and annoy us, and to pray for all.[6] This combination of corporal and spiritual almsdeeds turns out to be a good exposition of ministry, or service, to others.

Churches often appeal for "sacrificial" giving, that is, giving more than just ten percent or more than comes from the surplus we might have after meeting our own needs. But what is really needed is *sacramental giving*—that is, giving that brings grace.[7] Maimonides (Moses ben Maimon, 1135–1204), a medieval Jew, defined charity's eight degrees by ranking them brilliantly, starting with the lowest:

1. A person gives, but only when asked by the poor.
2. A person gives, but is glum when giving.
3. A person gives cheerfully, but less than he should.
4. A person gives without being asked, but gives directly to the poor. Now the poor know who gave them help and the giver, too, knows whom he has benefited.
5. A person throws money into the house of someone who is poor. The poor person does not know to whom he is indebted, but the donor knows whom he has helped.
6. A person gives his donation in a certain place and then turns his back so that he does not know which of the poor he has helped, but the poor person knows to whom he is indebted.
7. A person gives anonymously to a fund for the poor. Here the poor person does not know to whom he is indebted, and the donor does not know whom he has helped.
8. But the highest, he said, is this: Money is given to prevent another from becoming poor, such as providing him with a job or by teaching him a trade or by setting him up in business so he is not forced into the dreadful alternative of holding out his hand for charity. This is the highest step and the summit of charity's golden ladder.[8]

This eighth degree of giving is being done today in a major way. Microeconomic development, loaning small amounts of money to the poor to start little businesses, has been transformative for millions of people in the world. But we also need to do what Brian Griffiths and Kim Tan are doing, as proposed earlier, and that is to support midsized enterprises that will, when taxes are paid, provide resources for governments in the majority world to improve infrastructure, education, and health care. They propose fighting poverty through enterprise.[9]

More Blessed to Give Than to Receive

The heart dimension of giving is critical. Here are some factors:

- Do we recognize that we do not ultimately own what we are giving and therefore are charged with being good trustees?
- Are we thankful for what we have?
- Are we able to pay our taxes with a glad and generous heart, knowing that some of it, at least some, is helping our neighbors and enabling the government to provide infrastructure, health, and education benefits?
- Are we able to give to people or organizations with "no strings attached"—that is, trusting that it will be used wisely (we can do this through research) and not insisting on maintaining control over what is done with the money?
- And for Christians there must always be the willingness to "sell all" and follow Jesus if God calls us to do so.

All of this has a transforming effect on our souls. The soul is not a precious, immortal organ in an evil body, as the ancient Greeks often assumed, and as, sadly, many Christians believe today. The soul is the person, the longing person, the person reaching out to God, reaching out to ultimate reality and the meaning of life. We do not "have" souls; we "are" souls. And giving does something for the soul. Jacques Ellul is eloquent on this. He insists that money is

a power, part of the complex and usually invisible realities called
the "principalities and powers" (Eph. 6:12), those resistances to the
coming of God's kingdom that range from structures in society
(such as governments) to invisible spiritual realities, demons, and
even death itself, which, according to Scripture, holds people in
lifelong bondage.[10] And as a power, money makes a godlike claim
on us. But as Jacques Ellul so clearly shows, when we give money, we
disenfranchise it.[11] We strip money of its negativity, its radioactive
charge, its godlike appeal, and we transform it into a sacrament, a
means of grace to others and even ourselves.

In this matter of stewardship the church needs to take the lead
as an exemplary steward. But are we doing it?

The Church's Stewardship

John Stackhouse Jr., in reviewing the use of money in Christian
history, notes that there have been many attitudes toward giving
through the ages, ranging from prizing wealth as a blessing from
God, to renouncing wealth, especially for clergy who embraced a
kind of involuntary poverty. Stackhouse notes that the Reformation
started five hundred years ago with the rejection of using money to
buy indulgences—freedom from time in purgatory. The money raised
went to rebuild St. Peter's basilica in Rome. Could a sinner really offer
money to the church in lieu of acts of penance? Stackhouse continues, "Martin Luther's famous ninety-five theses were provoked by
indulgence-selling. Thus the Reformation, one might say, began over
a fundraising dispute."[12] But what is involved in giving?

Instead of asking what proportion of our money should be given
to God's purposes, we can learn to ask what amount of God's money
should we keep for ourselves? Richard Foster observes, "The difference
between these two questions is of monumental proportions."[13]

The church's use of time, the church's use of the gifts and talents of its members, and its allocation of financial resources make

a graphic statement about the church's stewardship. If the local church consumes all the discretionary time of its members, not freeing them for family and neighbors, if a church uses all its money on itself (staff and building), it is *hoarding*. If a church fails to release spiritual and natural gifts and allows people to "waste" themselves, it is *squandering*. So, what would it mean for the local church to invest as a steward in the kingdom of God?

Here are some specific suggestions to consider: Spend half of the church budget beyond the local church. Apply simple-living guidelines to the church and not just to individuals. Invest time, abilities, and finances in serving God's unity mission by linking poor and rich churches, Third World and Western churches, fighting injustice and bringing peace, working for unity and equality, as Paul did in the great collection (2 Cor. 8–9). Devote leadership and resources to supporting people where God has placed them in the world, rather than enlisting them for the programs of the church. Send groups of people (and not just checks) to care for the poor at home and abroad (remember Aquinas's blend of corporal and spiritual alms). But there is one area that is controversial and needs to be unpacked: the financial support of missionaries and people in professional Christian service.[14]

Financial Support of Christian Workers

From the point of view of not-yet Christians, raising money to support Christian workers—sometimes in extravagant lifestyles—smacks of religious hucksterism and may "hinder the gospel" (1 Cor. 9:12). Some people are required by nondenominational agencies to raise their own support. But when they do so, they feel they are forced to sell themselves. On the other hand, Scripture solidly endorses the financial support of some Christian workers to fulfill their particular ministries. The way in which this is done can be either upbuilding or destructive for the person supported, the people whose support is enlisted, and the watching world. This is a personal issue for both of us authors. Clive is a self-supported (tentmaking) theological educator. Paul has been a supported pastor and a supported theological educator but also a self-supported (tentmaking) pastor and a self-supported educator.

More than any other part of the New Testament, the letters of Paul deal with financial support. In 1 Corinthians 9, Paul defends the right of apostles like him (and by implication some other Christian workers) to be financially supported by Christians. His arguments are from the words of the Lord Jesus (1 Cor. 9:14), the practice of Jews and Gentiles in supporting people who work in their temples (v. 13), the law (which provides for the ox that is treading out the grain (vv. 8–9), and the everyday principle that people should expect to be supported by their labor (v. 7). But then Paul explains why he refuses to exercise his rights as an apostle and chooses to serve as a tentmaker. Tentmaking refers, in the case of the apostle Paul, to the practice of earning his living through work in the world, such as making tents, which was Paul's occupation, while serving generously in the church. But why would Paul do this? It has to do with two things: the advance of the gospel, which Paul believes is better served by being publicly free of personal financial gain and obligation to others, and Paul's own spiritual desire to preach the gospel free of charge as a love gift (compare Acts 18:1–3). We should remember that it was in Corinth that Paul had his most difficult time. He was accused of wrongdoing and misunderstood because most traveling philosophers received patronage with all its attendant obligations—"he who pays the piper calls the tune." Paul's overall concern is for the gospel. This tentmaking approach, however, was not something Paul always practiced.

Paul did receive financial support from the Philippian church, which is all the more remarkable because of its extreme poverty (2 Cor. 8:2), though he did so reticently, as shown by what has been called his "thankless thank you" (Phil. 4:14–19). There is no indication that Paul received their gifts during the time he was serving them or that he ever received support from other people while he was among them. In Ephesus, Paul ministered for two years (Acts 19), supporting himself by the work of his hands (Acts 20:33–34) in order to "help the weak" (v. 35). Paul concluded his work in Ephesus quoting the words of Jesus that it is more "blessed to give [in this context, giving ministry free of charge] than to receive [the gifts of people]" (v. 35). In Thessalonica, he also toiled day and night so as not to be a burden (1 Thess. 2:9) but to be a model to those with poor attitudes toward work (2 Thess. 3:8–10). We do not know what Paul did in Galatia, though he taught the principle of mutual ministry (Gal. 6:6)—which does not necessarily imply financial support, though this principle is mentioned in 1 Timothy 5:17–18. He received support from the Philippians when he was in Thessalonica (Phil. 4:16).

What does all this mean for us today? First, we are dealing with grace, not with law. No one should press for his or her rights to be supported. In the same way, no church should require all of its workers to be tentmakers by refusing to support their elders, who are worth, in Paul's language, a "double honor" (1 Tim. 5:17–18, the word used is the one used for the physician's honorarium).

Second, while being supported is an occasional privilege for Christian workers—perhaps one in one hundred—there is no mandate for people to go out seeking their own support; indeed, the spirit of the entire New Testament seems to point in the opposite direction toward doing all one can so as not to be a burden on others. It is the responsibility of the church to discern and call forth people to serve in a supported way. In other words, the call to be supported (unlike the call to ministry) does not come directly from God but comes from the people of God, who graciously free some to serve as supported workers.

Third, while there seems to be little justification for the almost universal practice today in parachurch agencies of sending people out to raise their own support, there is a strong case to be made for people *raising support for others*, as Paul did by his teaching and his aggressive fundraising for the poor saints in Jerusalem (1 Cor. 16:1–4; 2 Cor. 8–9) and his hard work to support his ministry colleagues. One constructive approach to the contemporary dilemma is for a person being led into a raise-your-own-support enterprise to prayerfully seek the counsel and help of the elders of their church and people who have known them for some time. If these people are unwilling or unable to raise support for the person, the Bible clearly mandates what to do. Those seeking support are not to send out letters begging for support or crisscross the country with their hands out; they are to work (1 Thess. 4:11–12; 2 Thess. 3:6–13).

Fourth, Paul's practice and teaching suggest the need for flexibility from place to place and time to time during one's lifetime. In some situations, the advance of the gospel is better served by refusing support and working as tentmakers; in other places, it would be better served by being supported. The world will never be reached or fully served if we rely completely on supported Christian workers. Though it is the almost universal assumption of the seminary system, it is highly questionable whether one should ever make a lifelong career out of supported Christian ministry.

The money is not ours. Being stewards gives meaning to our lives and helps us make sense out of everyday life. It captures all our energies, assets, and creativity for God's grand plan of humanizing the earth and developing it as a glorified creation. It saves us from the twin dangers of despair (What will come of the earth?) and false messianism (If we do not save the planet, who will?) because we are cooperating with a God who is determined to bring the creation and the peoples of the world to a worthy end through "the renewal of all things" (Matt. 19:28; Rev. 21:5). Stewardship is a thermometer of our spirituality and discipleship. Where our treasure is, there will be our hearts (Luke 12:34). Our response to a brother or sister in need is a measure of our love for God (James 2:15–16; 1 John 3:17). But stewardship also provides an incentive to grow in Christ. If we give sparingly, we will live cramped, emaciated lives; if we give generously, we live expansively and deeply. Jesus said, "Give, and it will be given to you. A good measure, pressed down, shaken together and running over, will be poured into your lap. For with the measure you use, it will be measured to you" (Luke 6:38). But that verse has been grossly misunderstood as a get-rich formula and leads us to the subject of the next chapter: the health and wealth gospel.[15]

9

The Health and Wealth Gospel

What makes every heresy dangerous is its element of truth.

Randy Alcorn[1]

It is arguable that materialism is the single biggest competitor with authentic Christianity for the hearts and souls of millions in our world today, including many in the visible church.

Craig L. Blomberg[2]

On November 20, 2015, after 140 days of trial proceedings which began in May 2013, all six accused church leaders, along with their families, arrived in a Singapore court in good spirits to hear the verdict. The lead pastor of City Harvest Church and his team of five leaders were charged with absconding with fifty million Singapore dollars (US$37 million) from church funds.[3] The money had been used to advance the secular music career of the lead pastor's wife. The criminal investigation started in 2010, and the case is the largest embezzlement of charity funds in the history of Singapore. City Harvest Church was started in 1989 and at its peak had a membership of thirty thousand. And lots of money. For example, in 2010, City Harvest Church stunned the public when that church announced that they had budgeted 310 million Singapore dollars (US$230 million) to take a significant stake in Suntec Convention Centre, a major commercial convention and shopping center in Singapore.[4]

Many of the church's supporters had queued overnight for a coveted pass into the courtroom, and they waved and cheered at the six as they walked into the court room. All six were found guilty and given prison sentences of seven months to three and a half years.[5] The long-drawn-out trial brought into the consciousness of Singaporeans a contemporary form of Christianity called the prosperity gospel. This so-called Christian movement became popular in the second half of the twentieth century and continued unabated as the fastest growing Christian movement in many parts of the world.

Source 1: *The American Dream*

Kate Bowler, a Canadian who researches what she calls "divine money," refers to "the prosperity gospel [as] a wildly popular Christian message of spiritual, physical, and financial mastery that dominates not only much of the American religious scene but some of the largest churches around the globe."[6] In the United States, the prosperity gospel is not confined only to Pentecostal churches but is found in other Christian denominations, the Latino churches, and the so-called black churches. Bowler traces the American landscape and history and argues how money, health, and good fortune become almost divine among American Christians. The movement sprang up in the late nineteenth century, flowered in the Pentecostal revivals during the World War II years, and matured in the individualism of post–1960s America. So what is it?

The prosperity gospel is an ongoing transformation of popular Christian imagination that amalgamates the gospel with the quest of the American Dream. Bowler claims, "It represent[s] the triumph of American optimism over the realities of a fickle economy, entrenched racism, pervasive poverty, and theological pessimism that foretold the future as dangling by a thread."[7] The American quest for fulfillment is realized through positive confession, the word of faith, and speaking words of health, wealth, and happiness into your life. It is constantly fed by consumer advertising that stokes discontent with your health, possessions, looks, and success. The American focus on traits like optimism and individualism tends to encourage a lofty view of human potential. "The prosperity gospel says you are good and have the ability to bend circumstances to your will. Simply change your thinking and your words, believe, and then God—your personal cosmic bellhop—will give you a push on the road to success," says commentator Russell Woodbridge.[8] In addition, major widely-read journals have provided commentary on the movement.

The September 2006 *Time* magazine carried a front cover that read, "Does God Really Want You to Be Rich?"[9] It showed the front of a Rolls Royce with a cross as an emblem, rather than the signature *Spirit of Ecstasy*, with wings and outstretched arms. According to *Time*, the good news of the prosperity gospel movement is that God does not want us to wait for the promised good life if we are bold enough to claim it. Known also as "Word of Faith, Health, and Wealth, Name It and Claim It, Prosperity Theology—its emphasis is on God's promised generosity in this life and the ability of believers to claim it for themselves."[10] If God really loves us then he would not want us to be broke. It is a very extensive movement.

In a poll in the same issue of *Time*, 17 percent of Christians identified themselves as part of such a movement, and 61 percent agreed that God wants people to be prosperous. Another 31 percent believed that God will bless you with more money if you give generously. John 10:10 in the King James Version could be considered this gospel's hallmark verse: "I have come that they may have life, and that they may have it more abundantly."

The prosperity gospel is proclaimed by some of the largest churches in the United States through the internet, television, and radio; it reaches millions of people around the world every day. Joel

Osteen, who was interviewed in the September 2006 *Time* magazine article, claims in his website that he reaches one hundred million households in the United States and tens of millions more in one hundred nations. Every week more than one million people access Osteen's website and download audio and video podcasts, making it one of the largest podcasts in the world. Joyce Meyer's "Enjoying Everyday Life" television program is aired in over ninety-five different languages and claims a potential audience of 4.5 billion around the world. Given the prosperity gospel's sharp deviation from the historical and orthodox message of the church, one would expect most Christians to reject it, but instead its popularity has been growing. David Jones and Russell Woodbridge comment that "This new gospel is perplexing—it omits Jesus and neglects the cross."[11] They note how this new message has overshadowed the gospel of Christ because it "has an appealing but fatal message: accept God and He will bless you—because you deserve it."[12] But there are other sources of this gospel besides the American Dream.

Source 2: The New Thought Movement

The New Thought movement is the philosophical root of the prosperity gospel. Emanuel Swedenborg (1688–1772) was a Swedish scientist and inventor who believed that he possessed the power to access heaven, hell, and other dimensions of the spiritual world. Through his writings he propagated ideas such as, "God is a mystical force, the notion that the human mind has the capacity to control the physical world, and the teachings of a works-based self-salvation scheme—ideas that later became core doctrines of New Thought," claim Jones and Woodbridge.[13] Swedenborg is considered the "grandfather of New Thought."[14] The New Thought movement began in the nineteenth century and came to be known by other names like Mind-Cure, Mental Healing, or Harmonialism. The International New Thought Alliance dates back to 1899 when groups of

New Thought advocates came together for a convention in Boston, Massachusetts. The Alliance encourages new members to join them in their dedication "to the spiritual enlightenment and transformation of each individual and the world."[15] "'Life is consciousness,' that leads one to the ever unfolding idea that in order to effect a change in our life, the realm of mind called consciousness must first change."[16] This is not a new idea. Earlier forms of similar philosophy were found in Gnosticism and Platonism, both of which believe that ideas depict reality.

Bowler, the Canadian researcher mentioned earlier, draws out three distinctive aspects of New Thought that insinuate and germinate within the framework of Christianity. First is the unity between God and humanity. Christian "salvation" is not an act of God alone but rather a divine act that draws out humanity's potential. Second, the world is reconfigured as thought rather than substance. Absolute reality is the spiritual world. The material world is the mind's projection. Third, New Thought argues that by means of thought we can share in God's power to create. Our worlds are shaped by our thinking, just as God created the world using thought. Positive thoughts yield positive outcomes, and negative thoughts yield negative circumstances. "These three features—a high anthropology, the priority of spiritual reality, and the generative power of positive thought—formed the main presuppositions of the developing mind-power," claims Bowler.[17] The well-known American psychologist and philosopher William James noted in 1905 the popularity of New Thought in American culture. "The mind-cure principles are beginning so to pervade the air that one catches their spirit at second hand. One hears of the 'Gospel of Relaxation,' of the 'Don't Worry Movement,' of people who repeat to themselves 'Youth, health, vigor!' when dressing in the morning."[18] According to James, New Thought is a combination of pagan philosophies found in Hinduism, philosophical idealism, transcendentalism, popular science evolution, and the optimistic spirit of progress.

As the world became modernized and industrialized, our pace of life quickened and we came to expect things to happen quickly. A sense of confidence and optimism about the potential of the human race encouraged a pragmatic self-mastery or self-help that allowed germs of the New Thought's ideas to develop into Positive Thinking.

Source 3: Positive Thinking

Positive thinking flourished in the years following World War II with the burgeoning consumer culture. It is frequently mistaken for optimism, but in reality it leaned on monism and philosophical idealism, mixing groups of religions with psychology and medicine. It developed as a "self-help" and "how-to" popular psychology that defined how life rewards those with right thinking. "By the 1950s, mindpower, recast as positive thinking, earned a lasting place in the popular religious imagination and the American prosperity movement," claim Jones and Russell.[19] Among its advocates is the Baptist minister and lawyer Russell H. Conwell (1843–1925), whose speech "Acres of Diamonds" was given more than six thousand times.[20] Conwell influenced later positive thinkers like Norman Vincent Peale, Robert Schuller, and Bruce Baton. In 1952, Norman Vincent Peale, who was the pastor of Marble Collegiate Church in New York City, published *The Power of Positive Thinking*, a *New York Times* bestseller that sold a million copies. Bowler observes that Peale's popularity in America was timely because of the rise of therapeutic culture. His "theological synthesis of upward mobility with religious buoyancy matched the postwar mood, turning a man into a movement."[21] Peale advocates a simple formula, "picturize, prayerize, and actualize."[22]

Positive thinking appeals to those looking for business success and riches, and it generated a new genre of American success literature. "To get rich, one needed to think one's way to wealth through the power of the mind, a notion which appealed to some American

business people," claims researcher Dawn Hutchinson.[23] Napoleon
Hill (1883–1970), a journalist and an aspiring businessman, so im-
pressed the industrialist Andrew Carnegie (1835–1919), that he was
commissioned to conduct a twenty-year study of 504 of America's
most successful people to derive a success formula for the average
person. As a result of this study, he wrote the bestselling classic,
Think and Grow Rich (1938). The most famous quote attributed to
Hill is, "Whatever the mind can conceive and believe the mind can
achieve."[24] In a 2010 email interview, Christina Chia, a contemporary partner of Napoleon Hill Associates in Malaysia, admitted that
Hill was influenced by New Thought thinkers like Ralph Waldo Em-
erson (1803–1882), Grison Swett Marden, William James (1842–1910),
and likely Charles Eillmore, Ernest Holmes, Henry Wood (1869–
1944), and Ralph Waldo Trine.[25] But it was not all about money.

Virtue is also important for the successful businessperson: knowledge, imagination, organized planning, and persistence are essential.
"Dreams come true when desire transforms them into concrete action."[26] Donald Meyer, in his study of positive thinkers, observes that
character became the enduring focus. It was a revival of the Protestant work ethic in which religious ideals are combined with practical
values, which "supplement[ed] the standard 'religious' virtues of faith,
hope, charity, etc., with the 'secular' virtues of industry, thrift, honesty,
practicality, rationality, and the like."[27] Unlike New Thought success
literature, which is geared toward a Christian audience, business literature gradually moved away from the religious rhetoric of prosperity
and adopted a more neutral language of success and riches. But we
need to ascertain the exact teaching of the prosperity gospel.

The Basic Teaching

Two names, E. W. Kenyon (1867–1948) and Kenneth E. Hagin
(1917–2003), are recognized by scholars as founders of the modern prosperity gospel movement. Most of the movement's teach-

ings in the last hundred years are attributed to them. Here is how they combined their efforts. Kenyon insinuated New Thought into the Christian theological framework through his writings, while Hagin popularized the prosperity gospel through the Word of Faith movement.

"Kenyon is the *primary* source of the health and wealth gospel of the independent Charismatic movement," claims Dale Simmons.[28] Kenyon founded Bethel Bible College in 1900 in Spencer, Massachusetts. He later moved to Washington state and founded the New Covenant Baptist Church and a radio program, *Kenyon's Church of the Air.* "His newsletter *Herald of Life* and the Seattle Bible Institute began there. Apart from *The Father and His Family* and *The Wonderful Name of Jesus,* Kenyon published most of his major works during this period," as Bowler notes.[29]

Hagin was the founder of the Word of Faith movement that is responsible for bringing the teachings of the prosperity gospel across the United States. The Word of Faith movement came of age in the 1970s as an esoteric form of positive Christian confession to achieve money, health, and victory. He founded Rhema Bible Training Center in 1962 and published the *Word of Faith* magazine together with various books reflecting the ideas of Kenyon. Hagin claimed that Jesus appeared to him personally and dictated the message: "Say it. Do it. Receive it. Tell it."[30]

Robert Bowman Jr., the author of *The Word-Faith Controversy,*[31] aptly summarizes the core beliefs of the Word of Faith movement, which we broadly classify here. First, it has a high regard for humans as God's creation to be themselves gods. And since God spoke the world into existence, we have the same power if only we speak with enough faith. Second, Jesus died not only physically but spiritually as well, and he was reborn in hell. Third, there continue to be "anointed" apostles and prophets today. Although they may not have the same authority as the canon of Scripture, they continue to receive revelations from Jesus or the Holy Spirit. Fourth, God has freed us from the curse of the law and we are now freed from all disease and poverty as well. "One simply needs to 'claim' the blessings of health and prosperity, just as one claims forgiveness of sins, because these are the rights of all Christian believers. Anyone who continues to be sick has simply not believed God's word."[32] The above beliefs of the Word of Faith movement shaped the contemporary prosperity gospel.

Bowler spent decades visiting and studying proponents of the prosperity gospel. She observes that it centers on four themes: faith, wealth, health, and victory.

> (1) It conceives of faith as an activator, a power that unleashes spiritual forces and turns the spoken word into reality. (2) The movement depicts faith as palpably demonstrated in wealth and (3) health. It can be measured in both the wallet (one's personal wealth) and in the body (one's personal health), making material reality the measure of the success of immaterial faith. (4) The movement expects faith to be marked by victory. Believers trust that culture holds no political, social, or economic impediment to faith, and no circumstance can stop believers from living in total victory here on earth.[33]

One of the prosperity gospel's favorite verses regarding wealth and giving is Malachi 3:10, in which God promises to "throw open the floodgates of heaven and pour out so much blessing that you will not have room enough for it." This happens when we bring the whole tithe to God's house. However, God was speaking through Malachi to a broken and spiritually impoverished Israel, telling the degenerate Jews to obey God in tithing and supporting the temple. Another favorite verse is 2 Corinthians 9:6, which argues that those who "sow generously will also reap generously." This verse is used to encourage generous tithing in order to receive generous reward. Those who give sparingly will live sparingly. Robert Tilton's "Law of

Compensation," according to Jones and Woodbridge, is based on a formula. "Christians need to give generously because when they do, God gives back more in return. This, in turn, leads to a cycle of ever-increasing prosperity."[34] You are not merely compensated, it is claimed, but compensated exponentially.

Further, Jesus's parable of the sower is used as a financial calculus of returning "thirty, sixty, or even a hundred times what was sown" (Mark 4:20). Gloria Copeland encourages her readers to focus on the hundredfold return and advises them to let these words grow by meditating and thinking about it regularly. "You give $1.00 for the gospel's sake and the full hundredfold return would be $100. Ten dollars would be $1,000. A hundredfold return on $1,000 would be $100,000."[35] She stresses, "When we receive offerings into this ministry, we believe for the hundredfold return to come back to those who give."[36]

Among the prosperity gospel's favorite verses regarding health is John's greeting to Gaius, "that you may enjoy good health and that all may go well with you" (3 John 1:2). New Testament scholar Gordon Fee comments that "good health" and "things to go well" for the recipients "was the standard form of greeting in a personal letter in antiquity."[37] On another favorite verse, John 10:10 in the King James Version about living abundant lives for believers of Jesus, Fee retorts that "'life, and have it to the full' has nothing to do with material abundance. 'Life' or 'eternal life' in John's Gospel is the equivalent of the 'kingdom of God' in the Synoptics [Matthew, Mark, and Luke]. It literally means the 'life of the Age to Come.'"[38]

On the theme of faith, the prosperity gospel refers to a "whole host of texts that remind us that God honors faith, e.g., Matthew 9:29; Mark 11:23–24; Hebrews 11:6; James 1:6–8."[39] The quest for perfect health lies in healing as a part of the atonement. In fact, we can demand our healing because God has provided for it; all we need is the right formula for faith. The emphasis is therefore on raising our faith. First Peter 2:24 and Isaiah 53:5 are frequently used to remind the followers that "by his wounds we are healed" (Isa. 53:5). Joyce Meyer, a popular prosperity preacher and writer, refers to Isaiah 53:3–4 to claim "pain cannot successfully come against my body because Jesus bore all my pain."[40] Fee argues that "the citation of Isaiah 53:5 in 1 Peter . . . do[es] not refer to physical healing. . . . 'Healing' here is a metaphor for being restored to health from the sickness of their sins."[41] Not surprisingly, biblical scholars are not the only people who have spoken against the movement.

Outcries against the Prosperity Gospel

In early 2015, a six-minute video was posted on the Creflo Dollar Ministries website, seeking "200,000 people committed to sow $300 or more [to] help achieve our goal to purchase the G650 airplane." Creflo Dollar, a high living prosperity gospel preacher at his Atlanta-area World Changers Church International, needed the $65 million Gulfstream jet so that he could "safely and swiftly share the Good News of the Gospel worldwide." Dollar believes he is entitled to whatever he wants. Dollar told his listeners, "If I want to believe God for a $65 million plane, you cannot stop me. You cannot stop me from dreaming. I'm gonna dream until Jesus comes." The board of World Changers Church agreed with him and announced the money had been raised and they were going ahead with the purchase: "A long-range, high-speed, intercontinental jet aircraft is a tool that is necessary in order to fulfill the mission of the ministry."[42] Ironically, Jesus's means of transport was a mule, and he borrowed it instead of raising money to buy it.

Michael Horton in his book, *Christless Christianity*,[43] observes that Americans are not known to blush. During the times of Judah's unfaithfulness, Jeremiah cried out against the false and lying prophets that tried to soothe the people. "Are they ashamed of their detestable conduct? No, they have no shame at all; they do not even know how to blush . . ." (Jer. 6:15). Paul wrote to the Corinthians to defend himself against false teachers and confronted them on being gullible:

> For if someone comes to you and preaches a Jesus other than
> the Jesus we preached, or if you receive a different spirit from
> the Spirit you received, or a different gospel from the one you
> accepted, you put up with it easily enough. (2 Cor. 11:4)

Unfortunately, false teachers know our weaknesses, "For such people are not serving our Lord Christ, but their own appetites. By smooth talk and flattery they deceive the minds of naive people," says Paul (Rom. 16:18). Such teachers are willing to tell exactly what people want to hear (2 Tim. 4:3–5). Smooth talk and flattery sell. Horton says, "no secular self-help guru comes close to the sales of evangelical rivals"[44] like Norman Vincent Peale and Robert Schuller in the past, and now Joel Osteen and Joyce Meyer.

Rick Warren, a pastor of a megachurch that does not subscribe to the prosperity gospel, offered a stinging criticism of the movement. "This idea that God wants everybody to be wealthy," snorts Warren, "there is a word for that: baloney. It's creating a false idol. You don't measure your self-worth by your net worth. I can show you millions of faithful followers of Christ who live in poverty. Why isn't everyone in the church a millionaire?" In the *Time* magazine interview, Milmon Harrison of the University of California at Davis, author of the book *Righteous Riches*, often sees the prosperity gospel as "another form of the church abusing people so ministers could make money."[45] But the prosperity gospel will not go away as long as the quest for the American Dream continues. Another interviewee, Edith Blumhofer, late director of Wheaton College's Center for the Study of American Evangelicals, observes that Protestantism over time has quietly adopted the idea that "you don't have to give up the American Dream. You just see it as a sign of God's blessing."[46] The Puritans combined religious insecurity with hard work, thrift and honesty to create the Protestant work ethic. Contemporary Christians combined religious aspiration with optimism, upward mobility, materialism and well-being to create the prosperity gospel movement. Not surprisingly the movement has gone global.

The Globalization of the Prosperity Gospel

Globalization has made the American Dream and middle-class aspirations worldwide pursuits. Following in their path is the increasing adoption of the prosperity gospel by churches in the two-thirds world, especially among the poor, where it purports to offer hope and optimism.

In a Pew Forum survey of Pentecostals in ten countries covering America, Latin America, Africa, and Asia, respondents were asked whether God "will grant material riches if one has enough faith." The majority answer is a resounding yes. In Latin America 64 percent agree, in Africa 83 percent agree, and in Asia 82 percent agree.[47] Randy Alcorn, reflecting on prosperity and eternity, notes,

> The health and wealth gospel will thrive in North America, Western Europe, Korea, Japan, Singapore, and other economically progressive counties. Far from being a reflection of biblical teaching, prosperity theology is a product of our place and time, a reflection of our materialism and self-absorption.[48]

Sadly, it is not only in rich countries that the prosperity gospel is thriving. I (Paul) was interviewing a missionary in one of the poorest countries of the world. "What is your greatest challenge that you face in your work of sharing the good news of the kingdom of God?" I asked. She replied, "The health and wealth gospel." But in the next chapter we need to move from this reflection on gaining prosperity in this life as we consider the challenging and troubling word of Jesus, to store up treasures for ourselves in heaven, in other words, lasting wealth.

10

Investing in Heaven

*The future reign is already here but it is here in the way
yeast is, hidden in the massive lump of the world. What
are we to do? We are to knead eternity into the world
until it becomes inextricable from it and both share
the same destiny.*

John Haughey[1]

*Command [those who are rich] to do good, to be rich
in good deeds, and to be generous and willing to share.
In this way they will lay up treasure for themselves as
a firm foundation for the coming age, so that they may
take hold of life that is truly life.*

The apostle Paul (1 Tim. 6:17–19)

I (Paul) was invited to speak at a faith and work conference in a
large Asian city. But a wealthy, local businessperson who bankrolled
many of the supported Christian workers in the city demanded that
he would speak, and speak first. He said his subject would be: "How
to Get Rich. And Quickly!" I had to follow that. My stomach was
churning. I abstained from critiquing his message except to say:
"If you follow Jesus you may become poorer." Often there is a dollar
cost for Christian people in business. So in the last chapter, we explored the complicated question of whether faith in Jesus will nor-

mally lead to wealth and health *in this life*. It is complicated partly because of the way Jesus responds to Peter's comment, "We have left everything to follow you!" (Mark 10:28). To this Jesus answers, in effect, that what is important is the spiritual kin that you acquire as a large family of God, "a new community of those who share with one another" (10:29–30).[2] In this chapter we are taking the longer look. We are asking whether we can invest *in the next life*, in heaven. And how? Not surprisingly, some people throughout history have thought it meant investing in the church here and now.

When Christianity became officially recognized in the fourth century, wealthy Christians increasingly put money into what they believed was a heavenly treasury—by giving money to build elaborate church buildings and, additionally, to help the poor. As the church became institutionalized, it was regarded as a religious transaction to bridge heaven and earth together in this way. Peter Brown, in his massive volume, *Through the Eye of a Needle*, documents how the Roman state flooded the economy with gold. Some of the gold went into church buildings. In response to the commercialization of religious giving, many people reacted and took to the desert, selling all, giving to the poor, living on pillars, or walling themselves up in caves. But the message from Christian North Africa was that "wealth was not to be thrown away in headlong renunciation; it was to be used in the churches. Above all, it was to be used to expiate sin."[3] But is this what it means, in the words of Jesus, to "store up for yourselves treasures in heaven" (Matt. 6:20)? It is freely and widely acknowledged that our treasure in heaven can be spiritual: knowing God as we are fully known (1 Cor. 13:12), standing as a pardoned person (Matt. 6:14), appropriating the full share of Christ's own peace and joy (John 14:27; 15:11), and having a calling that will never be revoked (Rom. 11:29). But can there be a material, earthy, and human inheritance in the next life?

We too often drop "new earth" from the promised future: "a new heaven and a new earth" (Rev. 21:1; Isa. 65:17). The truth is, there will be a great marriage—the merging of the invisible heaven with the visible creation as heaven comes to earth like a bride prepared for her groom (Rev. 21:2). It makes an enormous difference that the ultimate future of people and planet is the complete renewal of this world and this life, as well as the invisible world, as Scripture proposes (Rev. 21:5; Matt. 19:28), rather than the annihilation of this world and the construction of a wholly new one by God. Yves Congar, previously mentioned, puts it this way:

> Ontologically, this is the world that, transformed and renewed, will pass into the kingdom; so . . . the dualist position is wrong; final salvation will be achieved by a wonderful refloating of our earthly vessel rather than the transfer of the survivors to another ship wholly built by God.[4]

Toward this wonderful "refloating" the bodily resurrection of Jesus is a delicious foretaste not only of our own future but also the complete renewal of everything visible and invisible. But there is another foretaste: the irruption of the kingdom of God (sometimes called "the kingdom of heaven") into this life—that delightful rule of God bringing shalom, wholeness, human flourishing, and renewal.

So in this chapter we explore the connection between this life and the next particularly as it relates to money. Jesus uses two enigmatic phrases to describe lasting wealth: being "rich toward God" and "storing our treasure in heaven." Would that he had added, when he said this, "And this is what I mean by these phrases." We are left to ponder, to investigate, to ruminate on his other teachings and to research what this might mean. Which is exactly what we will do.

Rich toward God

This first phrase comes from a parable Jesus taught. Parables are life-pictures, most commonly from the marketplace, in which a single point is made, usually something about the kingdom of God. The story in Luke 12:13–21 is entitled "The Rich Fool" but the main character certainly did not look foolish. He was entrepreneurial and developed his agricultural business so that it yielded an abundant harvest. He was industrious—there is nothing wrong with making money so long as you do not love money. He was a steward—there is nothing wrong with taking care of your possessions rather than letting them rot, provided you are not possessed by them. In the story, we enter his business life as he is probably speaking to his servants. "I will tear down my barns and build bigger ones and there I will store my surplus grain" (v. 18). Next, we get inside his thought life. "I'll say to myself, 'You have plenty of grain laid up for many years. Take life easy; eat, drink and be merry'" (v. 19). But then God speaks to him: "You fool! This very night your life will be demanded from you. Then who will get what you have prepared for yourself?" (v. 20). One thing is certain: death reveals what we have been ultimately living for. The context of the parable is an incident that really happened. No imaginary story here.

Someone approached Jesus to solve a family inheritance problem: "Tell my brother to divide the inheritance with me" (v. 13). Sometimes an inheritance not only spoils descendants but divides them. Philip Marcovici notes that "any amount of wealth is enough to destroy a family."[5] And this is one of those sad cases. Jesus responds in a shrewd way. He avoids becoming triangulated into a dysfunctional family relationship and then gives a stern warning. "Watch out! Be on your guard against all kinds of greed; life does not consist in the abundance of possessions" (v. 15). The question was once asked, "How much is enough?" "Just a little more," is the answer attributed to John D. Rockefeller Sr. Then comes the story of the Rich Fool. So we can easily see what it means to think life consists in worldly wealth. "This is how it will be," says Jesus, "with whoever stores up things for themselves but is not rich toward God" (v. 21). But what does it mean to be "rich toward God"? Enter teaching number two, this time not in parable form but straight from the hip of Jesus.

Treasures in Heaven

"Do not store up for yourselves treasures on earth, where moth and rust destroy, and where thieves break in and steal. But store up for yourselves treasures in heaven, where moth and rust do not destroy, and where thieves do not break in and steal" (Matt. 6:19–20). Then Jesus goes for the jugular: "For where your treasure is, there your heart will be also" (v. 21). This is possibly the most personally challenging statement by Jesus on money and possessions. It comes in a context of what is called the Sermon on the Mount, a collection of sayings about life in the kingdom of God. Jesus continues with more gut-wrenching words. "No one can serve two masters. . . . You cannot serve both God and money" (v. 24). Some translations use the word "mammon" for money. This is followed by a long section on not worrying about food, drink, and clothing. He reminds his hearers that God dresses the flowers of the field magnificently, better than Solomon in all his splendor. Rather than worry, says Jesus, seek first God's kingdom and God's righteousness "and all these things will be given to you as well" (v. 33). Much of what Jesus did and said leads not to a pat answer but to a journey of exploration, heart-searching, and spiritual investigation. This one in particular.

John Haughey, in *The Holy Use of Money*, devotes an entire chapter to "mammonism." Haughey maintains that a major illness that pervaded the hearts of Jesus's listeners was this disease. The word "mammon" has the same root as "Amen," the word most people use to conclude their prayer with the meaning, "Let this be definite and secure." Mammon means that in which a person puts wholehearted trust. Scouring the teaching of Jesus, Haughey discerns three symptoms of this spiritually debilitating condition. First, people *run after things*. Anxiety is the root of this. Second, people experience *numbness.* The classic case is the rich man in Luke 16 who ignored the poor man Lazarus begging at his gate. Another example is shown by the priest and the Levite who passed by on the other side of the man fallen among thieves on the road to Jericho (Luke 10:25–37). Third, people suffering from mammonism have a *split consciousness.* These people have, or try to have, two masters: God and money.[6] The solution for this illness—once there is a diagnosis—is "Put your money in a different purse, a different treasury, a different bank account, one that moths can't get at and that cannot be stolen from you by anyone," says Haughey.[7] But this prompts deep and personal questions.

We must start by asking where our treasure is. Jesus said, "For where your treasure is, there your heart will be also" (Matt. 6:21). On what do we most rely? What is our greatest security? For what do we most long? What occupies our thoughts, dreams, and passions? Could we actually know that we have treasure in heaven? Of all the things we handle, what is most likely to last into eternity? These are probing questions. Whatever we discover through listening to our lives, through introspection, observation, or through the discernment of the Spirit, there is a way of preparing ourselves to invest in heaven.

Prerequisites for Investing in Heaven

I propose that our approach to gaining a heavenly treasure has two fundamental dimensions.

First, our consciousness—having a unitary vision. We saw that one of the symptoms of people who have a split consciousness— God and money—is doublemindedness. Jesus dealt with this in a short parable in Matthew that is embedded in the treasure-in-heaven teaching (Matt. 6:22–23) mentioned earlier. Using the metaphor of the eye, Jesus said that our faith, our life focus, is like the eye, which allows light in but does not see itself (except in a mirror).

If our eye is single, sound, or healthy, then our whole body is full of light. But, he warns, we must be careful that the light in us is not darkness. And how would we know that what we think of as light is in fact darkness? Here is how. We would not see clearly or holistically. When our faith/eye is sound, our whole bodily life will be enlightened—eating, sleeping, working, spending money, investing, relating, and functioning as a citizen and steward of creation. And how do we get this unitary vision that illuminates our whole life? By dedicating ourselves and everything we have to God along the lines of Romans 12:1–2—presenting our bodily life to God as a living sacrifice. But there is an even more effective way, the way of prayer.

The Psalms are the prayer book of the church. John Calvin called them "an anatomy of all the parts of the soul."[8] The Psalter explores human passion, hungers, and longings with incredible depth, so much so that one aspect of the Word of God in and through the Psalms is that you can *bring anything to God*: lament, sorrow, hunger, disaster, fear, sickness, thanksgiving, complaint (yes, even against God), satisfaction, and questions. God is revealed as one to whom we can tell the whole truth about everything. Praying the Psalms gives us a single view of everything under God, what we here call a unitary consciousness. In his powerful little book, *Psalms: The Prayer Book of the Bible*, Dietrich Bonhoeffer shows that the Psalms cover the universe and give us a unitary consciousness: creation, the law, holy history, the Messiah, the church, life, suffering, guilt, enemies, and the end.[9] But there is a second way through which we can gain an integrated approach to God and money—our thought life.

Second, a kingdom worldview. In *The Universe Next Door*, a classic work, James Sire defines worldview as follows.

A worldview is a commitment, a fundamental orientation of the heart, that can be expressed as a story or in a set of presuppositions ... which we hold (consciously or subconsciously,

consistently or inconsistently) about the basic constitution of
reality, and that provides the foundation on which we live and
love and have our being.[10]

A worldview is that story about everything that gives us meaning
and helps us make sense of life. It is the way we see everything, or
the lens through which we view everything. It affects how we think
and act. The dominant worldview that Jesus gives us to approach
life and the handling of money is the kingdom of God—the rule of
God in all of life, starting with the human heart. It is a worldview
that merges the material and spiritual. It merges this life and the
next, since the kingdom has already "come near" and is "among us"
right now, like a thin end of a wedge driven into this age. But there
is so much more to come when Christ returns and the kingdom of
God is consummated. So, with a kingdom worldview as we handle
money in this life we can be investing in the next life, since some of
our work, some of our relationships, some of our deeds, purged in
fire at the end, will find their place in the new heaven and new earth
(1 Cor. 3:10–15; 2 Pet. 3:10, 13). Haughey speaks of this worldview with
eloquence, referring to how Jesus looked at his life in this world.

> The kingdom of God, for Jesus, was not a spacey, spiritualized
> other world. It was composed of things in this world, but *focused
> differently*, seen in their relationship to the immediate, compas-
> sionate, powerful presence of the Father of Jesus. . . . Once a per-
> son took on Jesus' field of vision, he was susceptible to the trans-
> valuation of every single coin he would ever again possess.[11]

What is the shape of a kingdom worldview? A Christian worldview reflects the values of the kingdom of God. For example, in the
Magnificat sung by Mary—the really big people are the little ones
(Luke 1:46–55). This worldview reflects the lifestyle and values of
the Sermon on the Mount (Matt. 5–7)—especially the Beatitudes.

It enables us to pull back normal, "visible" reality to see what is really going on—cosmic spiritual warfare, God's ultimate reign, and the spiritual resources we have for life and work in the world. The Revelation, the last book in the Bible, is how the world looks to a person in the Spirit. And in a Christian worldview, dualism is displaced by full integration. "Spiritual work" (such as that of a pastor or missionary) is not more holy or acceptable to God, or even intrinsically more lasting, than homemaking, business, law, and trades. All are doing "the Lord's work." Work undertaken with faith, hope, and love will last, and purged of sin it will find its place in the new heaven and new earth. We get this worldview by immersing ourselves in the words of the New Testament. But there are also actions we can take.

Investing in Heaven—Four Redemptive Actions

First, we can invest in the kingdom of heaven/God through the relational use of our money. We have already considered in a previous chapter how relationships can transcend death. The parable in Luke 16:1–9 contains the strange word of Jesus that we are supposed to make friends for ourselves by means of worldly wealth so that when the wealth disappears (through our death), those friends will welcome us into their eternal habitations. What a grand rendezvous that will be! Another example is the great collection that Paul raised as he tramped through the gentile world. It was not for church buildings or even for the support of Christian workers. It was direct financial relief for the poor Jewish believers in Jerusalem and Judea who had lost their jobs and homes through becoming disciples of Jesus. First Corinthians 16 and 2 Corinthians 8 and 9 are all about this. Romans 15:27 reveals what was actually going on, what Paul's vision was for this money gift: the relatively rich Christians in the gentile world were giving some of their wealth to the materially poor Christians in the Jewish world. But the Jewish Christians were contributing from their own wealth—the law, prophets, the Messiah, and their spiritual blessings. And the purpose of this collection was to facilitate unity and equality (2 Cor. 8:14), a rich unity born of diversity and interdependence. And what is the treasure in heaven if we contribute to building unity and equality among the people of God? It is this: participating in an amazing multitude "from every nation, tribe, people and language" standing with the Lamb in the new heaven and new earth (Rev. 7:9). But there is more.

Second, we can invest in the kingdom of heaven/God through almsgiving to help the poor. In the chapter on social transformation, we considered how this can be accomplished through direct relief, microeconomic development, and medium-sized enterprises to assist people with employment and the dignity of work. We affirm this without being fully able to describe the shape and nature of that treasure. Perhaps there will be commerce in the new heaven and new earth, as hinted in the novel by George MacDonald, *The Curate's Awakening*. MacDonald describes all kinds of exchange taking place in the new heaven and new earth but without the passing of money! "How can these happy people do their business without passing a single coin?" to which he received the answer: "Where greed and ambition and self-love rule, there must be money; where there is neither greed nor ambition nor self-love, money is useless."[12]

Perhaps the treasure in heaven from almsgiving and stewardship will be in the form of flourishing, blessing, and wonderful relationships. Jesus calls this "your inheritance, the kingdom prepared for you since the creation of the world" (Matt. 25:34). But along with the inheritance of place, people, and the presence of God, we make a wonderful but surprising discovery. The Lord will say: "You fed me. You clothed me. You visited me." In the Parable of the Sheep and Goats, the righteous people on Jesus's right side are totally surprised that their gratuitous love for the poor and marginalized (because they did not see Jesus wearing the mask of the poor) was actually a ministry to Jesus. "Lord, when did we see you hungry and feed

you?" (v. 37), they ask.[13] This is matched by the surprise of the unrighteous people who protest that if they had known that they could
be serving and loving Jesus directly while they served and loved the
poor, they would gladly have fed, clothed, welcomed, and visited the
marginalized and vulnerable. But there is another way in which we
can invest in heaven, which we have addressed more fully in *Work
Matters*,[14] here abstracted: work that lasts.

*Third, we can invest in the kingdom of heaven/God through our
work done "in and for the Lord."* This is counter-church culture. Popular "Christian" belief claims that this whole world is going up in
smoke while the saints will be evacuated from it to enjoy a spiritual
future in a brand new creation wholly made by God. But why would
God destroy what he has lovingly made? In contrast with this pes-
simistic view of work and creation, the Christian view of the future
is that God refloats this earthly vessel wholly renewed rather than
transferring the survivors and their work to another lifeboat. How
could this be? There are several biblical reasons for this hope: the
resurrection of Jesus, the continuity of the picture of the next life
with this life, and the passages that proclaim that our labor in the
Lord will last, including 1 Corinthians 13:13: "these three remain:
faith, hope, and love."[15]

In 1 Corinthians 15:58, at the end of his exposition of the practical
implications of Jesus's resurrection and our future resurrection, Paul
exhorts the Corinthians, "Always give yourself fully to the work of
the Lord, because you know that your labor in the Lord is not in
vain." Admittedly, Paul's first reference in this passage to "the work
of the Lord" points to the various ministries engaged in by the Co-
rinthian believers. But even these included such things as "helping"
and "administrating." In a wider application of the chapter, Paul
is assuring his friends that what makes all their labor—whether
homemaking or bridge-building—worthwhile and enduring is the
fact that it is done "in the Lord." Speaking to this hopeful text, Alan
Richardson, in a pioneering theology of work, comments: "It is in

the resurrection of Christ that we find the final vindication of all the work that we do in this life, our assurance that our toil and struggle and sufferings possess abiding worth: the short 'six days' of our working life on earth will be crowned with that heavenly rest wherein we will survey our work and see that it is good."[16] So how does this happen?

John Haughey says, "The future reign is already here but it is here in the way yeast is, hidden in the massive lump of the world. What are we to do? We are to knead eternity into the world until it becomes inextricable from it and both share the same destiny."[17] But there is a final dimension to investing in heaven and having treasure in heaven.

Fourth, our ultimate treasure in this life and even more so in the next is Christ. Haughey admits that "to say 'someone is my wealth' brings us into the strange world of metaphor because of the conjoining of different realities whose link is not immediately evident."[18] But it is a truth that the apostle Paul relished. In Philippians 3:7–11 Paul says, "Whatever were gains to me I now consider loss for the sake of Christ. What is more, I consider everything a loss because of the surpassing worth of knowing Christ Jesus my Lord, for whose sake I have lost all things. I consider them garbage, that I may gain Christ and be found in him. . . . I want to know Christ—yes, to know the power of his resurrection and participation in his sufferings . . . and so, somehow, attaining to the resurrection of the dead." If we have begun to know him in this life, enjoy his presence, find him to be life itself as well as the way and the truth, how much more will we know him when we see him face to face, and know as we, in this life, are known? In some translations Philippians 3:8 is rendered, "That Christ may be my wealth" (NAB). There is no greater treasure.

Lesslie Newbigin, speaking for many in his generation, says, "We are without conviction about any worthwhile end to which the travail of history might lead."[19] Not so. In fact, we have a glorious future and can even contribute to the furniture of the new heaven and new earth. Money is part of this, although whether we will use money in the new heaven and new earth is an open question. But our use of money now can contribute to our ultimate future when "the kingdom [fully] comes" and "the will of God is done on earth as it is in heaven." N. T. Wright says about this phrase from the Lord's Prayer, "That remains one of the most powerful and revolutionary sentences we can ever say."[20]

I (Paul) have heard many of the great living preachers in the world today. I confess I cannot remember anything they said. But I do remember a sermon I heard as a teenager from a pastor in a small church, who was certainly not famous. He said you can do with your life what you do with money. You can squander it, wasting it away like the prodigal son. Or, he said, you can hoard it, wrap it up in a handkerchief, and just keep it intact. Or, he said, you can invest it. And today I am inviting you to invest your life in Christ and his kingdom. So, we conclude along with this pastor, let money be invested for and in the kingdom of God now and forever.

Questions for Reflection and Discussion

Introduction

1.   Which of the questions in the last paragraph (on money and the kingdom of God) most engages you?
2.   What other question do you bring to this book that you would like to discuss in a group or with your friends and family?

Chapter 1: Growing Up without Money

1.   Jacob Needleman's statement says that to study money is to study ourselves. What do you think your relation to money says about you?
2.   The apostle Paul, speaking to those with money, says, "Command those who are rich in this present world not to be arrogant nor to put their hope in wealth, which is so uncertain, but to put their hope in God, who richly provides us with everything for our enjoyment" (1 Tim. 6:17). What do you think Paul would say to those who grow up without money?
3.   What did you learn about money from your family in your growing-up years?
4.   Honestly reflect on how often your decisions are driven by money rather than prayer and Christian values. Why do you think this is so?

Chapter 2: Growing Up with Money

1.   What do you think about Paul's distinction (as he reflects on his father) that you can love *making* money without *loving* money?

2.   Paul tells the story of growing up next door to extreme poverty and the effect this had on him. Today we mostly live in silos and get connected with the other half via media. What would be a better way of relating to people in extreme need?

3.   "Children should not have to save up for their parents, but parents for their children" (2 Corinthians 12:14). The apostle Paul is arguing that his own unwillingness to be a financial burden to the Corinthians is like the principle of parents providing for their children. In this chapter we called this the "Western" way. What do you think it really means in any culture?

4.   For fun draw a lifeline horizontally with a block every ten years (1–10, 11–20, 21–30, etc.) and on the vertical axis draw another line to indicate how important money was to you in each decade. Why the variation?

Chapter 3: Holy Money

1.   Does it matter whether we view money as merely a neutral medium of exchange or as power? If so, why?

2.   How do you respond to the chapter's argument that money had a "sacred" beginning, rooted in the temples?

3.   How do you react to the statement that money has a "soul"?

4.   Read Ephesians 6:10–17 about the principalities and powers, those visible and invisible forces that make it hard for us to

live and work righteously. Money, it is argued, is a "power." All things were created good (Col. 1:15–16) but have become corrupted, but ultimately the corrupt will be overpowered by Christ (Col. 2:13–15). As we live life in the "messy middle" (between the first coming of Jesus and final renewal of everything), how can we practically regard money as something valued but not sacred?

Chapter 4: Giving to God and Caesar

1. Revisit Matthew 22:15–22. Why do you think Jesus teasingly left unexplained his profound statement to "give to God" what God deserves? Why do you think most people understand this to mean giving money to church ministries, missions, or charitable ventures? What is good about this? What is not so good?

2. What factors leading to dualism (the idea that some things are sacred and some things secular) are at work in your own culture?

3. A kingdom worldview integrates life (including our handling of money) into a single reality of grace from God. Would it be true to say that Jesus turns money from being a problem into a sacrament—a spiritual grace through a physical means? How?

Chapter 5: Grappling Shrewdly with Capitalism

1. How could something so good—the rise of capitalism and its enormous productivity—be fraught with so many negative side-effects?

2. Do you see any evidences of a "gracious capitalism" in spite

of the global spread of the situation of the "rich man and the poor man" in the parable of Jesus (Luke 16:19–31)?

3.   How do you react to Craig Gay's suggestion that we should not work for the capitalist system *per se* but work in it for fellowship with God and neighbor?

4.   "Money flattens all values and makes all decisions and objects comparable on a monetary basis." So what?

5.   How do you respond to the assertion that capitalism has become a religion?

Chapter 6: How to Buy Forever Friendships

1.   Have you had any experiences of having your friendship "bought," or have you seen money used to gain a friend? Describe the situation.

2.   So what is problematic with using money to build relationships? What could be good about it?

3.   In the parable of the dishonest manager (Luke 16:1–15), the master's clients knew the person who had relieved their debt. In so many charitable situations today there is no personal connection between giver and receiver. Do you see this as a problem or a blessing? Why?

4.   The manager in this parable is commended for acting shrewdly with the boss's money (Luke 16:8). Most commonly, *shrewdness* in handling money is considered negatively, shot through with personal cunning and self-interest. But how could shrewdness be a good approach to our handling of money? (See also Matt. 10:16.)

5.   Think of several ways of using money to care for others which may have the byproduct of building forever friendships. Describe them.

Chapter 7: Why Money "Talks"

1. How do you see money affecting social relationships, both positively and negatively? Be as descriptive as possible.
2. What evidence do you have that in your own life you have "tagged" money for various social purposes? Have you encountered "good" and "bad money" (sacred and profane)? What have you done about this?
3. Revisit the story in Judges 17:5–6 of Micah's transforming the money he had stolen and returned into an idol, thereby mixing the sacred and profane. Do you see this kind of thing happening today, and how? If idolatry is making something other than God one's ultimate concern, what makes people worship money today?
4. How do you react to the statement that "money talk is a man's talk"? Do you agree that women tend to view money differently than men? If so, why? If not, why?
5. Is talking about money a taboo in your social circles? If so, why? If not, why?
6. How do you answer Viviana A. Zelizer's question: "When does money enhance moral concerns and sustain social lives? Under what conditions does monetization advance justice and equality?"

Chapter 8: Whose Money Is It Anyway?

1. What were you taught in the church about money, if you were taught anything? About stewardship? Where does this come from? Scripture? Church culture? Contemporary culture?
2. Jacques Ellul argues that when we give money away we *disenfranchise* money. We strip money of its negativity, its ra-

dioactive charge, its godlike appeal and transform it into a sacrament, a means of grace to others and even ourselves. Are there other ways we can disenfranchise money?

3.   The chapter argued that moving from sacrificial giving to sacramental giving has an effect on our souls. How do you see this happening?

4.   The concluding section on supporting Christian workers is counter to the prevailing Christian culture. Do you think it is a needed correction? If not, why not?

5.   Meditate on the text, "'The silver is mine and the gold is mine,' declares the LORD Almighty" (Haggai 2:8). What does the text say to you?

Chapter 9: *The Health and Wealth Gospel*

1.   Do you believe that God wants every Christian to be rich? Why do believe as you do?

2.   What is true about the teaching of the health and wealth gospel? What is not true? On what basis would you assign some parts as true and edifying and other parts as dangerous?

3.   Read the most-quoted texts of the health and wealth gospel in their context: Malachi 3:10; Mark 4:20; 3 John 1:2; John 10:10; Isaiah 53:5. Put these in the context of the whole teaching of the Bible, especially the kingdom of God that is here now (but only partially) and yet coming fully at the end time. How does the health and wealth gospel lead people to embrace a false hope in their current life? What does this do to living by faith, including having faith in the unseen (Hebrews 11:1, 13), as we are called to in Scripture?

Chapter 10: Investing in Heaven

1.   Paul says in 1 Timothy 6:17–19, "Command [those who are rich] to do good, to be rich in good deeds, and to be generous and willing to share. In this way they will lay up treasure for themselves as a firm foundation for the coming age, so that they may take hold of life that is truly life." In what way can such generosity lay up a foundation for us in the life to come?

2.   Most contemporary Christian leaders make statements about "going to heaven," especially at funerals and memorials. What radical difference does it make to say our ultimate future is not to be merely immortal souls in heaven but to be fully resurrected persons in a "new heaven and a new earth" (Revelation 21:1)?

3.   What practical difference does it make to say that this world will *not* be annihilated when the end time comes but wonderfully transformed and transfigured?

4.   In Matthew 6:21 Jesus goes for the jugular: "For where your treasure is, there your heart will be also." Where is your treasure? (Perhaps the questions raised in the chapter may help in this reflection.)

5.   The kingdom of God, God's coming new world that is centered in Jesus, gives us a "unitary vision" in contrast to a split consciousness and double-mindedness. What practical steps can you take to gain this kingdom worldview (and life-view), especially as it relates to money?

6.   What have you personally learned and imbibed from this book and the questions and reflections at the end of each chapter?

Notes

Introduction

1. Quoted in Jeffrey K. Salkin, *Being God's Partner: How to Find the Hidden Link between Spirituality and Your Work* (Woodstock, VT: Jewish Lights Publishing, 1994), 145.

2. Jacob Needleman, *Money and the Meaning of Life* (New York: Doubleday, 1991), 112.

3. See also Proverbs 23:4–5; 28:20; 30:8–9; Psalm 49:6–7; Hosea 12:8.

4. Craig L. Blomberg, *Neither Poverty nor Riches: A Biblical Theology of Possessions* (Downers Grove, IL: InterVarsity Press, 1999), 83. Emphasis his. Blomberg masterfully examines the biblical material on wealth and poverty.

5. Blomberg, *Neither Poverty nor Riches*, 145.

6. For a full treatment of the kingdom of God, see R. Paul Stevens, "The Kingdom of God: Biblical Research," available through Institute for Marketplace Transformation, paul@imtglobal.org.

7. Blomberg, *Neither Poverty nor Riches*, 113.

8. Bruce K. Waltke, *An Old Testament Theology* (Grand Rapids: Zondervan, 2007), 209.

Chapter 1

1. Melissa West, "Tie Your Camel to the Hitching Post: An Interview with Jacob Needleman," http://www.personaltransformation.com/jacob_needle man.html.

2. Saint Augustine, *Confessions*, trans. Henry Chadwick (Oxford: Oxford University Press, 1991), Book V, 87, Para. 23. Augustine came to Milan from Rome to fill a position for a rhetoric teacher. It was in Milan that he heard Bishop Ambrose's preaching, " . . . known throughout the world as among the best of men, devout in your worship."

3. Augustine, *Confessions*, Book V, 88, Para. 23. Though Augustine was bored and contemptuous of God, he was drawn by Ambrose's preaching.

4. Jacob Needleman, *Money and the Meaning of Life* (New York: Doubleday, 1991).

5. Needleman, *Money and the Meaning of Life*, 206.

6. Quoted in West, "Tie Your Camel to the Hitching Post."

Chapter 2

1. Søren Kierkegaard, *Papers and Journals*, trans. Alastair Hannay (New York: Penguin, 1996), 161.

2. Kierkegaard, *Papers and Journals*, p. 161.

3. imtglobal.org.

4. 1 Timothy 5:8 about providing for your own relatives can be taken both ways, providing for your parents and providing for your children.

Chapter 3

1. John Maynard Keynes, *Treatise on Money* (New York: Harcourt, Brace, 1930), II, 28992, quoted in Norman Oliver Brown, *Life against Death: The Psychoanalytical Meaning of History* (Middletown, CT: Wesleyan University Press, 1985), 247.

2. William Goetzmann, *Money Changes Everything: How Finance Made Civilization Possible* (Princeton, NJ: Princeton University Press, 2016), 100.

3. Glyn Davies, *A History of Money: From Ancient Times to the Present Day*, (Cardiff: University of Wales Press, 2002), 48.

4. Goetzmann, *Money Changes Everything*, 44

5. Sociologist Emile Durkheim argues that society is the source of religion. The sacred beliefs and practices developed in a community because of the need for emotional stability in communal living. Please refer to Emile Durkheim, *The Elementary Forms of Religious Life*, trans. Karen E. Fields (New York: Free Press, 1995).

6. Goetzmann, *Money Changes Everything*, 22.

7. Goetzmann, *Money Changes Everything*, 49.

8. Karl Polanyi, *The Great Transformation: The Political and Economic Origins of Our Time* (Boston: Beacon, 2001), 48.

9. Bernhard Laum, *Heiliges Geld* (Tübingen: Mohr, 1924), 880, quoted in Brown, *Life against Death*, 246.

10. Alla Semenova, "The Origins of Money: Evaluating Chartalist and Metallist Theories in the Context of Ancient Greece and Mesopotamia" (PhD diss., University of Missouri–Kansas City, 2011), ii, https://mospace.umsys tem.edu/xmlui/bitstream/handle/10355/10843/SemenovaOriMonEva.pdf. Of interest in terms of the history of the names for coins, the meat in these sacrificial feasts was roasted on a broach, which was called *obelos* in Greek. According to Laum, this was the root of the coin name *obolos*. So from this roasted bull flesh on sacrificial roasting spits (*obeloi*) the concept of money evolved and, finally, became coins, which initially had served as a symbolic representation of roasted bull's meat.

11. Jan Sokol, "Money and the Sacred: B. Laum's Hypothesis on the Origins of Money," (lecture, Center for the Study of World Religions, Harvard University, Cambridge, MA, October 1, 2008).

12. John Maynard Keynes, *Treatise on Money* (New York: Harcourt, Brace, 1930), II, 28992, quoted in Brown, *Life against Death*, 247.

13. David Graeber, *Debt: The First 5,000 Years* (New York: Melville House, 2012), 21–41.

14. Adam Smith, *The Wealth of Nations* (New York: Bantam Classic, 2003), 33.

15. Smith, *The Wealth of Nations*, 33.

16. Caroline Humphrey, "Barter and Economic Disintegration," *Man* 20: 48–72, as quoted in Graeber, *Debt*, 29.

17. Graeber, *Debt*, 34.

18. Graeber, *Debt*, 37.

Chapter 4

1. Jacob Needleman, *Money and the Meaning of Life* (New York: Doubleday, 1991), 51.

2. Eusebius of Caesarea, *Demonstration of the Gospel*, quoted in W. R. Forrester, *Christian Vocation* (New York: Scribner's, 1953), 43. Emphasis added.

3. Craig L. Blomberg notes that "Between the more than 23.3% of goods that had to be paid in Jewish tithes, the temple tax and other occasional or freewill offerings, and the additional tribute to Rome, the average Jew in the early first century labored under a tax burden that ranged from roughly 30% to 50% of his total income." *Neither Poverty nor Riches: A Biblical Theology of Possessions* (Downers Grove, IL: InterVarsity Press, 1999), 89.

4. R. T. France, *Matthew*, Tyndale New Testament Commentaries (Grand Rapids: Eerdmans, 1985), 314.

5. N. T. Wright, *Matthew for Everyone*, Part 2 (London: SPCK, 2002), 87.

6. France, *Matthew*, 315.

7. France, *Matthew*, 315.

8. See how Yves Congar prepared the way for the radical rediscovery of the dignity and ministry of nonclergy members of the people of God through Vatican II by showing in Scripture that prince, prophet, and priest were not pope, bishop, and parish priest but the whole believing community. Yves M. J. Congar, *Lay People in the Church: A Study for a Theology of the Laity*, trans. D. Attwater (Westminster, MD: Newman Press, 1957).

9. I. Howard Marshall, "How Far Did the Early Christians Worship God?," *Churchman* 99, no. 3 (1985).

10. Needleman, *Money and the Meaning of Life*, 167.

11. See Lee Hardy, *The Fabric of This World* (Grand Rapids: Eerdmans, 1990).

12. Quoted in Max Stackhouse et al, *On Moral Business: Classical and Contemporary Resources for Ethics in Economic Life* (Grand Rapids: Eerdmans, 1995), 39.

13. Quoted in Gordon Preece, "Business as a Calling and Profession: Towards a Protestant Entrepreneurial Ethic" (unpublished manuscript delivered at the International Marketplace Theology Consultation, Sydney, June 2001), 14.

14. Karl Barth, "Vocation," in *Church Dogmatics*, III/4 (Edinburgh: T&T Clark, 1961), 601, quoted in Paul Marshall, *A Kind of Life Imposed on Man: Vocation and Social Order from Tyndale to Locke* (Toronto: University of Toronto Press, 1996), 22.

15. Some of the above is abstracted from R. Paul Stevens, *Doing God's Business: Meaning and Motivation for the Marketplace* (Grand Rapids: Eerdmans, 2006), 40–59.

16. Martin Luther, *Luther's Works*, American Edition, 55 vols., ed. Jaroslav Pelikan (St. Louis: Concordia, 1955–86), 36:78.

17. Max Weber, *The Protestant Ethic and the Spirit of Capitalism* (Mineola, NY: Dover Publications, 2003).

18. Gianfranco Poggi, *Calvinism and the Capitalist Spirit: Max Weber's Protestant Ethic* (London: Macmillan, 1983), 61.

19. Guy Oaks, "The Thing That Would Not Die: Notes on Reflection," in *Weber's Protestant Ethic: Origins, Evidence, Contexts*, ed. Hartmut Lehmann and Guenther Roth (New York: Cambridge University Press, 1993), 241.

20. Poggi, *Calvinism*, 79. Emphasis added. While Poggi argues that the set of conditions Weber described were not *sufficient* to account for the rise

of capitalistic entrepreneurship, Weber described "a *necessary* part" in these phenomena. The multiple factors essential for a capitalistic economic system to emerge from feudalism are considered in Brian Griffiths, *The Creation of Wealth: A Christian's Defense of Capitalism* (Downers Grove, IL: InterVarsity Press, 1985), 94.

21. Griffiths, *The Creation of Wealth*, 31.

22. Craig Gay, *The Way of the (Modern) World: Or, Why It's Tempting to Live as If God Doesn't Exist* (Grand Rapids: Eerdmans, 1998), 140–41.

23. Gay, *The Way of the (Modern) World*, 145.

24. Gay, *The Way of the (Modern) World*, 153.

25. Georg Simmel, *The Philosophy of Money*, trans. Tom Bottomore and David Frisby (London: Routledge, 2004), 443–46.

26. In *Lady Windemere's Fan*, Oscar Wilde had Lord Darlington quip that a cynic was "a man who knows the price of everything and the value of nothing." As with so much of what Wilde wrote or said, it's more than just a nice turn of phrase—it hits at the heart of the problems of society. *Lady Windemere's Fan* was written in 1892, but what Wilde wrote is even more true now than it was more than 120 years ago.

27. William Perkins, *The Works of That Famous Minister of Christ in the University of Cambridge* (London: John Legatt, 1626), 754D.

28. Perkins, *The Works*, 555A.

29. Perkins, *The Works*, 555C.

30. See Calvin's secret call in R. Paul Stevens, *The Other Six Days: Vocation, Work, and Ministry in Biblical Perspective* (Grand Rapids: Eerdmans, 2000), 154.

31. R. H. Tawney, *Religion and the Rise of Capitalism* (Harmondsworth, UK: Pelican [Penguin Books], 1977), 248, quoted in Gay, *The Way of the (Modern) World*, 167. Gay also quotes Robert S. Michaelson, "Changes in the Puritan Concept of Calling or Vocation," *New England Quarterly* 26 (1953): 315–36.

32. See Klaus Bochmuehl, "Recovering Vocation Today," *Crux* 24, no. 3 (1988): 25–35.

33. *Initiatives, In Support of Christians in the World*, PO Box 291102, Chicago, IL 60629.

34. *Initiatives* 234 (September 2017): 1.

35. Paul Cho, "Overcoming Cultural Barriers for Korean Pastors Becoming Tentmakers" (unpublished ThM paper for Regent College, Vancouver, 2016). See also Tong-Shik Ryu, *The History and Structure of the Korean Shamanism* (Seoul: Yonsei University Press, 1983), 14–15; Sung-Gun Kim, "Pentecostalism, Shamanism, and Capitalism within Contemporary Korean Society," in *Spirits*

of Globalization: The Growth of Pentecostalism and Experiential Spiritualities in a Global Age, ed. Sturla J. Stalsett (London: SCM Press, 2006), 27.

36. Colin Lewis, "The Soul of Korean Christianity: How the Shamans, Buddha, and Confucius Paved the Way for Jesus in the Land of the Morning Calm" (a project for the University Scholars Program, Seattle Pacific University, 2014), 7.

37. Lewis, "The Soul," 10.

38. Andrew Powell, *Living Buddhism* (New York: Harmony Books, 1989), 28.

39. Young-hoon Lee, *The Holy Spirit Movement in Korea: Its Historical and Theological Development* (Oxford: Regnum Books International, 2009), 46.

40. Jason Mandryk, *Operation World* (Colorado Springs, CO: Biblica, 2010), 511.

41. France, *Matthew*, 315-16.

42. See John C. Haughey, SJ, *The Holy Use of Money: Personal Finance in Light of Christian Faith* (Garden City, NY: Doubleday, 1986).

Chapter 5

1. Craig M. Gay, *Cash Values: Money and the Erosion of Meaning in Today's Society,* (Grand Rapids: Eerdmans, 2004), 17.

2. Erich Fromm, *To Have or to Be?* (New York: Open Road Media, 2002), Kindle edition, 7.

3. According to Geoffrey Ingham, "this creation of credit-money by lending in the form of issued notes and bills, which exist independently of any particular level of incoming deposits, is the critical development . . . the *differentia specifica* of capitalism. *The Nature of Money* (Cambridge: Polity Press, 2004), 115, quoted in John Smith, "The Role of Money in Capitalism," *International Journal of Political Economy,* February 2002.

4. China embarked on free-market reforms in 1978 with agricultural reforms: Farmers were allowed to own land and grow any crop, and the selling price for agricultural produce was increased dramatically. In 1981, prices of industrial products were liberalized, and private enterprises were allowed to set up factories in rural areas. By the mid-1980s, a substantial portion of rural countryside had private farms and had developed basic industries.

5. The Berlin Wall was built in 1961 to divide East and West Berlin. Built by the Soviet-ruled portion of the city, the wall was meant to keep out Western "fascists." At twelve feet tall and four feet wide, the wall and its surrounding security systems were known as "The Death Strip."

6. Peter Berger, *The Capitalistic Revolution* (New York: Basic Books, 1986), 43.

7. Brian Griffiths, *The Creation of Wealth: A Christian's Defense of Capitalism* (Downers Grove, IL: InterVarsity Press, 1984).

8. Gay, *Cash Values,* 18.

9. Lawrence Mishel and Jessica Schieder, "CEO Compensation Surged in 2017 Report," *Economic Policy Institute,* August 16, 2018, https://www.epi.org/publication/ceo-compensation-surged-in–2017/. In the report it was found that in 2017, the CEO-to-average-worker compensation ratio was 312 to 1. It was a bumper year for the American corporate chieftains. The average CEO of one of the 350 largest firms in the US received $18.9 million in compensation, a 17.6% increase over 2016.

10. Utilitarianism emphasizes the maximization of utility, which is generally regarded as well-being of the people whose interest is considered. Refer to John Stuart Mill, *Utilitarianism,* Kindle ed. (Heritage Illustrated Publishing, 2014).

11. Michael Sandel, *What Money Can't Buy: The Moral Limits of Markets* (New York: Farrar, Straus and Giroux, 2012), 34.

12. Joseph Cropsey, "Adam Smith," in *History of Political Philosophy,* 3rd ed., ed. Leo Strauss Joseph Cropsey (Chicago: University of Chicago Press, 1987), 652, quoted in Gay, *Cash Values,* 53. Emphasis added.

13. "As to their (the "heathen") distance from us, whatever objections might have been made on that account before the invention of the mariner's compass, nothing can be alleged for it, with any colour of plausibility in the present age. . . . Yea, and providence seems in a manner to invite us to the trial, as there are to our knowledge trading companies, whose commerce lies in many of the places where these barbarians dwell. . . . Scripture likewise seems to point out this method, 'Surely the Isles shall wait for me; the ships of Tarshish first, to bring my sons from far, their silver, and their gold with them, unto the name of the Lord, thy God' (Isa 60:9)." William Carey, *An Enquiry into the Obligations of Christians to Use Means for the Conversion of the Heathens* (London: The Carey Kingsgate Press Ltd., 1792/1961), 67–68.

14. Brian Griffiths and Kim Tan, *Fighting Poverty through Enterprise: The Case for Social Venture Capital* (Coventry, UK: The Venture Centre, 2007), 5.

15. Caleb E. Finch, "Evolution of the Human Lifespan and Diseases of Aging: Roles of Infection, Inflammation, and Nutrition," *Proceedings of the National Academy of Sciences of the United States* 107: 1718–24 (January 26, 2010), https://www.pnas.org/content/107/suppl_1/1718/tab-article-info.

16. Michael Novak, *The Spirit of Democratic Capitalism* (New York: Simon & Schuster, 1982), 13, quoted in Gay, *Cash Values,* 18.

17. Nathan Rosenberg and L. E. Birdzell Jr., *How the West Grew Rich: The Economic Transformation of the Industrial World* (New York: Basic Books, 1986), 33, quoted in Gay, *Cash Values,* 25.

18. Jonathan Haidt, "How Capitalism Changes Conscience," *Center for Humans & Nature,* September 28, 2015, https://www.humansandnature.org /culture-how-capitalism-changes-conscience.

19. Ron Inglehart and Christian Welzel, *World Values Survey,* http://www .worldvaluessurvey.org/.

20. Inglehart and Welzel, *World Values Survey*; see section on Findings & Insights. For further reference, see Christian Welzel, *Freedom Rising: Human Empowerment and the Quest for Emancipation* (New York: Cambridge University Press, 2013).

21. Note in the following paper on entrepreneurship that the deepest motive for innovation arising from the Protestant Reformation is love and gratitude. See R. Paul Stevens, "The Spiritual and Religious Sources of Entrepreneurship: From Max Weber to the New Business Spirituality," *Crux* 36, no. 2 (June 2000): 22–33, reprinted in *Stimulus: The New Zealand Journal of Christian Thought and Practice* 9, no. 1 (February 2001): 2–11.

22. Gay, *Cash Values,* 98–99. Emphasis in original.

23. Zhao Xiao, interview by PBS, *Frontline World,* www.pbs.org/frontline world/stories/china_705/interview/xiao.html.

24. Paul Mason, *Postcapitalism: A Guide to Our Future,* Kindle ed. (New York: Farrar, Straus and Giroux, 2015), loc. 25.

25. The Organisation for Economic Co-operation and Development (OECD), *Policy Challenges for the Next 50 Years,* July, 2014, 10, https://www .oecd.org/economy/Policy-challenges-for-the-next-fifty-years.pdf.

26. Nick Srnicek and Alex Williams, *Inventing the Future: Postcapitalism and a World without Work,* rev., updated ed. (London: Verso Books, 2016), 103–10.

27. Jonathan Haidt, "Three Stories about Capitalism," *Righteous Mind* (blog), July 20, 2014, https://righteousmind.com/three-stories-about-capi talism/. Jonathan Haidt, a social psychologist at New York University's Stern School of Business, frequently discusses the morality of capitalism.

28. Robert Hahnel, *Of the People, by the People: The Case for a Participatory Economy* (Chico, CA: AK Press Distribution, 2012), 96–97.

29. Jacques Ellul, *Money and Power*, limited ed. (Eugene, OR: Wipf & Stock, 2009), 19.

Chapter 6

1. Daniel Draht, "Redeeming the Church's Understanding of Effectiveness in the Workplace" (unpublished paper in Marketplace Theology, Regent College, Vancouver, 2016), 3.

2. For a full treatment of the kingdom of God please see R. Paul Stevens, "The Kingdom of God: Biblical Research," available through Institute for Marketplace Transformation: paul@imtglobal.org.

3. N. T. Wright, *Luke for Everyone* (Louisville: Westminster John Knox, 2004), 196.

4. Draht, "Redeeming" 3.

5. Draht, "Redeeming," 5.

6. Craig L. Blomberg notes that the issue in first-century Judaism was "not one's socio-economic level *per se*, but the amount of honor or shame that accrued to a person. Thus, a wealthy steward who fell out of favor with his master was actually at greater risk than the average villager, since he could move all the way from the rich retainer class to the expendables and find himself literally in danger of starving to death." *Neither Poverty nor Riches: A Biblical Theology of Possessions* (Downers Grove, IL: InterVarsity Press, 1999), 102.

7. John Nolland, *Luke 9:21–18:34*, vol. 35B of *Word Biblical Commentary*, ed. David A. Hubbard, Glenn W. Barker, John D W Watts, and Ralph P. Martin (Dallas: Word, 1993), 799.

8. Draht, "Redeeming," 5.

9. Translated as *shrewd* in the New International Version, New Living Translation, and New American Standard Bible.

10. Translated as *wise* in the King James Version and New Revised Standard Version Bibles.

11. Translated as *innocent* in the New International Version, New Revised Standard Version, and New American Standard Bible.

12. Translated as *harmless* in the King James Version, New Living Translation, and New Revised Standard Version Bibles.

13. Draht, "Redeeming," 1–2.

14. Kenneth E. Bailey, *Poet & Peasant* and *Through Peasant Eyes: A Literary-Cultural Approach to the Parables in Luke* (Grand Rapids: Eerdmans, 1983), 86.

15. I. Howard Marshall, *Luke: Historian and Theologian* (Grand Rapids:

Zondervan, 1974), 142. Marshall notes how Jesus has "broadened out the time of the End so that it begins with the ministry of Jesus, includes the time of the church, and is consummated at the parousia [second coming of Jesus]." This time of fulfillment is an era of salvation in which the good news is preached to the poor, and the reversals of life take place—the poor, those literally dependent and oppressed, are saved, and the independent and self-righteous rich are not saved (121–24).

16. Wright, *Luke for Everyone,* 201.

Chapter 7

1. Viviana A. Zelizer, *The Social Meaning of Money: Pin Money, Paychecks, Poor Relief, and Other Currencies* (Princeton: Princeton University Press, 2017), 222.

2. Quoted in Bruce G. Carruthers, "The Meanings of Money: A Sociological Perspective," *Theoretical Inquiries in Law* 11, no. 1 (2010): 52. For further reference see George Herbert Mead, *Mind, Self, and Society* (1934).

3. Carruthers, "The Meanings of Money," 52.

4. Georg Simmel, *The Philosophy of Money*, 3rd ed. (New York: Routledge, 2004).

5. Simmel, *The Philosophy of Money*, 177.

6. Fernand Braudel, *The Structures of Everyday Life* (New York: Harper & Row, 1982), quoted in Carruthers, "The Meanings of Money," 55.

7. Joel Kaye, *Economy and Nature in the Fourteenth Century: Money, Market Exchange, and the Emergence of Scientific Thought* (Cambridge: Cambridge University Press, 1998), 16–17, 39, 53.

8. Thomas Carlyle, a nineteenth-century Scottish historian, was the first to use this word, but it was popularized by Karl Marx and Friedrich Engels in their writings in the fields of political economy and sociology.

9. Carruthers, "The Meanings of Money," 55.

10. Carruthers, "The Meanings of Money," 73.

11. Zelizer, *The Social Meaning of Money*, 1.

12. Zelizer, *The Social Meaning of Money*, 3.

13. Zelizer, *The Social Meaning of Money*, 3.

14. Zelizer, *The Social Meaning of Money*, 222.

15. Russell Belk and Melanie Wallendorf, "The Sacred Meanings of Money," *Journal of Economic Psychology* 11 (1990): 36.

16. Belk and Wallendorf, "The Sacred Meanings of Money," 37.

17. Belk and Wallendorf, "The Sacred Meanings of Money," 38.

18. Belk and Wallendorf, "The Sacred Meanings of Money," 62.

19. Liz Perle, *Money: A Memoir* (New York: Picador, 2006), 26.

20. Perle, *Money: A Memoir*, 28.

21. Perle, *Money: A Memoir*, 29.

22. Floyd W. Rudmin, "German and Canadian Data on Motivations for Ownership: Was Pythagoras Right?," paper presented at Association for Consumer Research conference, New Orleans, LA, October 19–22, 1989, quoted in Belk and Wallendorf, "The Sacred Meanings of Money," 51.

23. Viviana A. Zelizer, "On the Social Meaning of Money: 'Special Monies,'" *American Journal of Sociology* 95, no. 2 (September 1989): 342–77.

24. Michael J. Silverstein and Kate Sayre, "The Female Economy," *Harvard Business Review*, September 2009, https://hbr.org/2009/09/the-female-economy.

25. Adele Azar-Rucquoi, *Money as Sacrament: Finding the Sacred in Money* (Berkeley: Celestial Arts, 2002), intro.

26. Perle, *Money: A Memoir*, 13.

27. Perle, *Money: A Memoir*, 221.

28. Suzanne Woolley, "Your Credit Score Could Make or Break Your Love Life," *Bloomberg.com*, August 21, 2017, https://www.bloomberg.com/news/articles/2017-08-21/a-high-credit-score-can-make-you-look-sexy-on-dating-apps.

29. Woolley, "Your Credit Score."

30. Catey Hill, "This Number Could Predict Your Chances of Getting Divorced," *New York Post*, May 10, 2017, https://nypost.com/2017/05/10/this-number-could-predict-your-chances-of-getting-divorced/.

31. Hill, "This Number."

32. Viviana A. Zelizer, "Money, Power, and Sex," *Yale Journal of Law and Feminism* 18 (2006): 303, https://papers.ssrn.com/sol3/papers.cfm?abstract_id=944055.

33. Woolley, "Your Credit Score."

34. David W. Krueger, "A Self-Psychological View of Money," in *The Last Taboo: Money as Symbol and Reality in Psychotherapy and Psychoanalysis* (New York: Brunner/Mazel, 1986).

35. Adrian Furnham and Michael Argyle, *The Psychology of Money* (New York: Routledge, 2008), 3, quoted in Liezel Alsemgeest, "Talking about Money Is Taboo: Perceptions of Financial Planning Students and Implications for

the Financial Planning Industry," *Industry & Higher Education*, September 22, 2016, https://www.researchgate.net/publication/308570708.

36. Perle, *Money: A Memoir*, 17.

37. Gordon Redding, *The Spirit of Chinese Capitalism* (Berlin: de Gruyter, 1995), 39.

38. Redding, *The Spirit of Chinese Capitalism*, 73.

39. Redding, *The Spirit of Chinese Capitalism*, 71.

40. Chan Kwok Bun and Claire Chiang, *Stepping Out: The Making of Chinese Entrepreneurs* (Singapore: Prentice-Hall, 1995), 246.

Chapter 8

1. Quoted in Randy Alcorn, *Money, Possessions, and Eternity* (Carol Stream, IL: Tyndale, 1989), 205.

2. Much of this chapter is adapted from two articles written by R. Paul Stevens, "Stewardship" and "Financial Support," in *The Complete Book of Everyday Christianity*, ed. Robert Banks and R. Paul Stevens (Downers Grove, IL: InterVarsity Press, 1997), 962–67 and 419–22, respectively.

3. C. J. H. Wright, *God's People in God's Land: Family, Land, and Property in the Old Testament* (Grand Rapids: Eerdmans, 1990), 117.

4. R. T. France, "God and Mammon," *Evangelical Quarterly* 51 (1979): 18, quoted in Craig L. Blomberg, *Neither Poverty nor Riches: A Biblical Theology of Possessions* (Downers Grove, IL: InterVarsity Press, 1999), 145.

5. John Chrysostom, *On Wealth and Poverty*, trans. Catherine P. Roth (Crestwood, NY: St. Vladimir's Seminary Press, 1984).

6. Thomas Aquinas, "Treatise on Faith, Hope, and Charity," in *Summa theologiae* II-II, q. 32, art. 2.

7. For an exposition of this see Jacques Ellul, *Money and Power*, limited ed. (Eugene, OR: Wipf & Stock, 2009), 62–65. Ellul also argues that Christ "strips wealth of its sacramental character that we have recognized in the Old Testament" (70).

8. William E. Diehl and Judith Ruhe Diehl, *It Ain't Over Till It's Over* (Minneapolis: Augsburg, 2003), 129–30.

9. Brian Griffiths and Kim Tan, *Fighting Poverty through Enterprise: The Case for Social Venture Capital* (Coventry, UK: The Venture Centre, 2007).

10. Ellul, *Money and Power*, 75.

11. Ellul, *Money and Power*, 109.

12. John Stackhouse Jr., "Money in Christian History," *Vocatio* 5, no. 1 (August 2001): 17–20.

13. Richard J. Foster, *Money, Sex, and Power: A Challenge of the Disciplined Life* (San Francisco: Harper & Row, 1985), 35.

14. Resources for stewardship: John Chrysostom, *On Wealth and Poverty,* trans. Catherine P. Roth (Crestwood, NY: St. Vladimir's Seminary Press, 1984); Oscar E. Feucht, *Everyone a Minister* (St. Louis: Concordia, 1974); R. Foster, *Freedom of Simplicity* (New York: Harper & Row, 1989); D. J. Hall, *Stewardship of Life in the Kingdom of Death* (Grand Rapids: Eerdmans, 1988); L. T. Johnson, *Sharing Possessions: Mandate and Symbol of Faith* (London: SCM, 1981); M. MacGregor, *Your Money Matters* (Minneapolis: Bethany House, 1988); R. J. Sider, *Cry Justice: The Bible on Hunger and Poverty* (New York: Paulist, 1980); R. J. Sider, *Living More Simply: Biblical Principles and Practical Models* (Downers Grove, IL: InterVarsity Press, 1980); R. J. Sider, *Rich Christians in a Hungry World* (Dallas: Word, 1990).

15. Resources for financial support: R. Allen, *Missionary Methods: St. Paul's or Ours?* (Grand Rapids: Eerdmans, 1992); J. M. Bassler, *God and Mammon: Asking for Money in the New Testament* (Nashville: Abingdon, 1991); J. M. Everts, "Financial Support," in *Dictionary of Paul and His Letters,* ed. G. F. Hawthorne, R. Martin, and D. G. Reid (Downers Grove, IL: InterVarsity Press, 1993) 295–300; G. Georgi, *Remembering the Poor: The History of Paul's Collection for Jerusalem* (Nashville: Abingdon, 1992).

Chapter 9

1. Randy Alcorn, *Money, Possessions, and Eternity* (Carol Stream, IL: Tyndale, 1989), 103.

2. Craig L. Blomberg, *Neither Poverty nor Riches: A Biblical Theology of Possessions* (Downers Grove, IL: InterVarsity Press, 1999), 132.

3. Danson Cheong, "City Harvest Trial: Six Accused Guilty of All Charges," *The Straits Times,* October 22, 2015, https://www.straitstimes.com/singapore /courts-crime/city-harvest-trial-six-accused-guilty-of-all-charges.

4. Sharon Chen, "Singapore Mega-Church Christian Faithful Invest in Malls," *Bloomberg,* September 4, 2012, https://www.bloomberg.com/news /articles/2012-09-03/singapore-mega-church-faithful-invest-in-malls-south east-asia.

5. Huiwen Ng, "City Harvest Case: Is This the End of the Saga? Here's All You Need to Know," *The Straits Times,* February 1, 2018, https://www.straits times.com/singapore/courts-crime/city-harvest-case-recap-of-a-saga-that -dragged-on-for-7-years.

6. Kate Bowler, *Blessed: A History of the American Prosperity Gospel* (Oxford: Oxford University Press, 2013), 3.

7. Bowler, *Blessed*, 7.

8. Russell S. Woodbridge, "Prosperity Gospel Born in the USA," June 4, 2015, http://www.thegospelcoalition.org/article/prosperity-gospel-born-in-the-usa.

9. David Van Biema and Jeff Chu, "Does God Want You To Be Rich?," *Time*, Sept. 10, 2006, http://content.time.com/time/magazine/article/0,9171,1533448,00.html.

10. Van Biema and Chu, "Does God Want You to Be Rich?"

11. David W. Jones and Russell S. Woodbridge, *Health, Wealth, and Happiness: Has the Prosperity Gospel Overshadowed the Gospel of Christ?* (Grand Rapids: Kregel Publications, 2011), 14.

12. Jones and Woodbridge, *Health, Wealth, and Happiness*, 16.

13. Jones and Woodbridge, *Health, Wealth, and Happiness*, 29.

14. Martin A. Larson, *New Thought; or, a Modern Religious Approach: The Philosophy of Health, Happiness, and Prosperity* (New York: Philosophical Library, 1985), 6, quoted in Jones and Woodbridge, *Health, Wealth, and Happiness*, 29.

15. Larson, *New Thought*, 6.

16. "What Is New Thought?," International New Thought Alliance, https://newthoughtalliance.org/what-is-new-thought/.

17. Bowler, *Blessed*, 13–14.

18. William James, *The Varieties of Religious Experience* (London: Longmans, Green and Co., 1905), 95, quoted in Jones and Woodbridge, *Health, Wealth, and Happiness*, 28.

19. Jones and Woodbridge, *Health, Wealth, and Happiness*, 30.

20. Russell H. Conwell, *Acres of Diamonds* (Uhrichsville, OH: Barbour and Company, 1993), 31.

21. Bowler, *Blessed*, 56.

22. Norman Vincent Peale, *The Power of Positive Thinking* (New York: Fireside/Simon & Schuster, 2003), 55, quoted in Bowler, *Blessed*, 57.

23. Dawn Hutchinson, "New Thought's Prosperity Theology and Its Influence on American Ideas of Success," *Nova Religio: The Journal of Alternative and Emergent Religions* 18.2 (Fall 2014): 28–44, 38.

24. Hutchinson, "New Thought's Prosperity Theology," 40.

25. Hutchinson, "New Thought's Prosperity Theology," 40.

26. Napoleon Hill, *Think and Grow Rich* (Wise, VA: Napoleon Hill Foundation, 1937), 33.

27. Donald Meyer, *The Positive Thinkers: Popular Religious Psychology from Mary Baker Eddy to Norman Vincent Peale and Ronald Reagan* (Middletown, CT: Wesleyan University Press, 1988), quoted in Bowler, *Blessed*, 37.

28. Dale H. Simmons, *E. W. Kenyon and the Postbellum Pursuit of Peace, Power, and Plenty* (Lanham, MD: Scarecrow Press, 1997), xi, quoted in Jones and Woodbridge, *Health, Wealth, and Happiness*, 51.

29. Bowler, *Blessed*, 16.

30. Kenneth E. Hagin, *How to Write Your Own Ticket with God* (Tulsa, OK: Kenneth Hagin Ministries, 1979), 6–8, quoted in Jones and Woodbridge, *Health, Wealth, and Prosperity*, 55.

31. Robert M. Bowman Jr., *The Word-Faith Controversy: Understanding the Health and Wealth Gospel* (Grand Rapids: Baker, 2001).

32. Robert Bowman Jr., "Word of Faith Movement," *Profile, Watchman Fellowship*, https://www.watchman.org/profiles/pdf/wordfaithprofile.pdf.

33. Bowler, *Blessed*, 7.

34. Jones and Woodbridge, *Health, Wealth, and Happiness*, 65.

35. Gloria Copeland, *God's Will Is Prosperity: A Roadmap to Spiritual, Emotional, and Financial Wholeness* (Fort Worth, TX: Kenneth Copeland Publications, 1978), 65.

36. Copeland, *God's Will Is Prosperity*, 66.

37. Gordon Fee, *The Disease of the Health and Wealth Gospels*, Kindle ed. (Vancouver, BC: Regent College Publishing, 2006), loc. 77.

38. Fee, *The Disease of the Health and Wealth Gospels*, loc. 80.

39. Fee, *The Disease of the Health and Wealth Gospels*, loc. 252.

40. Joyce Meyer, "List of Confessions by Joyce Meyer," https://joycemeyer .org/everydayanswers/ea-teachings/list-of-confessions-by-joyce-meyer.

41. Fee, *The Disease of the Health and Wealth Gospels*, loc. 285.

42. Steve Siebold, "The Biggest Scam of All: Pastor Creflo Dollar Will Get His $65 Million Luxury Jet," June 2005, 2016, https://www.huffpost.com/entry /the-biggest-scam-of-all-p_b_7521170.

43. Michael Horton, *Christless Christianity: The Alternative Gospel of the American Church* (Grand Rapids: Baker, 2008), 65–66.

44. Horton, *Christless Christianity*, 67.

45. Van Biema and Chu, "Does God Want You to Be Rich?"

46. Van Biema and Chu, "Does God Want You to Be Rich?"

47. Pew Forum, "Spirit and Power: A 10-country Survey of Pentecostals," (Washington, DC: Pew Research Center, 2006), 147.

48. Alcorn, *Money*, 89.

Chapter 10

1. John C. Haughey, *Converting Nine to Five: A Spirituality of Daily Work* (New York: Crossroad, 1989), 104.

2. Craig L. Blomberg, *Neither Poverty nor Riches: A Biblical Theology of Possessions* (Downers Grove, IL: InterVarsity Press, 1999), 140.

3. Peter Brown, *Through the Eye of a Needle: Wealth, the Fall of Rome, and the Making of Christianity in the West, 350–550 AD* (Princeton: Princeton University Press, 2012), xx.

4. Yves M. J. Congar, *Lay People in the Church: A Study for a Theology of the Laity*, trans. D. Attwater (Westminster, MD: Newman Press, 1957), 92.

5. Philip Marcovici, *The Destructive Power of Family Wealth: A Guide to Succession Planning, Asset Protection, Taxation, and Wealth Management* (Hoboken, NJ: John Wiley & Sons Inc., 2016), 17.

6. John C. Haughey, *The Holy Use of Money: Personal Finance in Light of Christian Faith* (Garden City, NY: Doubleday, 1986), 10–16.

7. Haughey, *The Holy Use of Money*, 12.

8. John Calvin, *Commentary on the Psalms*, trans. James Anderson (Grand Rapids: Baker, 1996), Part 1, Vol. 1, xxxvii. He explains the reason for this insightful title:

> There is not an emotion of which any one can be conscious that is not here represented as in a mirror. Or rather, the Holy Spirit has here drawn . . . all the griefs, sorrows, fears, doubts, hopes, cares, perplexities, in short, all the distracting emotions with which the minds of men are wont to be agitated. The other parts of Scripture contain the commandments which God enjoined his servants to announce to us. But here the prophets themselves, seeing they are exhibited to us as speaking to God, and laying open all their inmost thoughts and affections, call, or rather draw, each of us to the examination of himself in particular, in order that none of the many infirmities to which we are subject, and of the many vices with which we abound, may remain concealed. It is certainly a rare and singular advantage, when all lurking places are discovered, and the heart is brought into the light, purged from that most baneful infection, hypocrisy.

9. Dietrich Bonhoeffer, *Psalms: The Prayer Book of the Bible* (Minneapolis: Augsburg, 1970), 27.

10. James W. Sire, *The Universe Next Door*, 4th ed. (Downers Grove, IL: InterVarsity Press, 2004), 17.

11. Haughey, *The Holy Use of Money*, 24, emphasis added.

12. George MacDonald, *The Curate's Awakening* (Minneapolis: Bethany House Publishers, 1985), 145.

13. Blomberg makes an insightful comment: "The slogan based on the passage, made particularly famous by Mother Teresa, 'seeing Jesus in the face of the poor,' irrespective of their religious commitment, therefore at best encapsulates only a partial truth and at worst is highly misleading." *Neither Poverty nor Riches,* 126.

14. R. Paul Stevens, *Work Matters: Lessons from Scripture* (Grand Rapids: Eerdmans, 2012), 154–66.

15. Haughey says: "It is not the pure intention alone, nor is it faith, hope and love residing unexercised as three infused theological virtues in a person that last. What lasts is the action taken on these virtues, the praxis that flows from the intention, the works the virtues shape. These last!" Haughey, *Converting Nine to Five*, 106.

16. Alan Richardson, *The Biblical Doctrine of Work* (London: SCM, 1954), 55–56.

17. Haughey, *Converting Nine to Five*, 104.

18. Haughey, *The Holy Use of Money*, 235.

19. Lesslie Newbigin, *Honest Religion for Secular Man* (Philadelphia: Westminster, 1966), 46.

20. N. T. Wright, *Surprised by Hope: Rethinking Heaven, the Resurrection, and the Mission of the Church* (New York: HarperOne, 2008), 29.

Selected Bibliography

Alcorn, Randy. *Money, Possessions, and Eternity*. Carol Stream, IL: Tyndale, 1989.

Aquinas, Thomas. "'Treatise on Faith, Hope, and Charity." In *Summa theologiae* II-II, q. 32, art. 2.

Azar-Rucquoi, Adele. *Money as Sacrament: Finding the Sacred in Money*. Berkeley: Celestial Arts, 2002.

Bailey, Kenneth E. *Poet & Peasant* and *Through Peasant Eyes: A Literary-Cultural Approach to the Parables in Luke*. Grand Rapids: Eerdmans, 1983.

Barth, Karl. "Vocation." In *Church Dogmatics*, III/4. Edinburgh: T&T Clark, 1961.

Bassler, J. M. *God and Mammon: Asking for Money in the New Testament*. Nashville: Abingdon, 1991.

Belk, Russell, and Melanie Wallendorf. "The Sacred Meanings of Money." *Journal of Economic Psychology* 11 (1990): 35–67.

Berger, Peter. *The Capitalistic Revolution*. New York: Basic Books, 1986.

Blomberg, Craig L. *Neither Poverty nor Riches: A Biblical Theology of Possessions*. Downers Grove, IL: InterVarsity Press, 1999.

Bochmuehl, Klaus. "Recovering Vocation Today." *Crux* 24, no. 3 (1988): 25–35.

Bonhoeffer, Dietrich. *Psalms: The Prayer Book of the Bible*. Minneapolis: Augsburg, 1970.

Braudel, Fernand. *The Structures of Everyday Life*. New York: Harper & Row, 1982.

Bright, John. *The Kingdom of God*. Nashville: Abingdon, 1953.

Brown, Norman Oliver. *Life against Death: The Psychoanalytical Meaning of History*. Middletown, CT: Wesleyan University Press, 1985.

Brown, Peter. *Through the Eye of a Needle: Wealth, the Fall of Rome, and the Making of Christianity in the West, 350–550 AD*. Princeton: Princeton University Press, 2012.

Calvin, John. *Commentary on the Psalms*. Translated by Rev. James Anderson. Grand Rapids: Baker, 1996.

Carey, William. *An Enquiry into the Obligations of Christians to Use Means for the Conversion of the Heathens*. London: The Carey Kingsgate Press Ltd., 1792/1961.

Carruthers, Bruce G. "The Meanings of Money: A Sociological Perspective." *Theoretical Inquiries in Law* 11, no. 1 (2010): 52.

Chan Kwok Bun and Claire Chiang. *Stepping Out: The Making of Chinese Entrepreneurs*. Singapore: Prentice-Hall, 1995.

Chrysostom, John. *On Wealth and Poverty*. Translated by Catherine P. Roth. Crestwood, NY: St. Vladimir's Seminary Press, 1984.

Congar, Yves M. J. *Lay People in the Church: A Study for a Theology of the Laity*. Translated by D. Attwater. Westminster, MD: Newman Press, 1957.

Cropsey, Joseph. "Adam Smith." In *History of Political Philosophy*, edited by Leo Strauss and Joseph Cropsey, 3rd ed. Chicago: University of Chicago Press, 1987.

Davies, Glyn. *A History of Money: From Ancient Times to the Present Day*. Cardiff: University of Wales Press, 2002. http://library.uniteddiversity .coop/Money_and_Economics/A_History_of_Money-From_Ancient _Times_to_the_Present_Day.pdf.

Diehl, William E., and Judith Ruhe Diehl. *It Ain't Over Till It's Over*. Minneapolis: Augsburg, 2003.

Draht, Daniel. "Redeeming the Church's Understanding of Effectiveness in the Workplace." Unpublished paper in Marketplace Theology. Regent College, Vancouver, 2016.

Durkheim, Emile. *The Elementary Forms of Religious Life*. Translated by Karen E. Fields. New York: Free Press, 1995.

Ellul, Jacques. *Money and Power*. Limited edition. Eugene, OR: Wipf & Stock, 2009.

Eusebius of Caesarea. *Demonstration of the Gospel*. Quoted in W. R. Forrester. *Christian Vocation*. New York: Scribner's, 1953.

Everts, J. M. "Financial Support. In *Dictionary of Paul and His Letters*, edited by G. F. Hawthorne, R. Martin, and D. G. Reid. Downers Grove, IL: InterVarsity Press, 1993.

Finch, Caleb E. "Evolution of the Human Lifespan and Diseases of Aging: Roles of Infection, Inflammation, and Nutrition." *Proceedings of the National Academy of Sciences of the United States* 107 (January 26,

2010): 1718–24. https://www.pnas.org/content/107/suppl_1/1718/tab
-article-info.

Foster, Richard J. *Money, Sex, and Power: A Challenge of the Disciplined Life.*
San Francisco: Harper & Row, 1985.

France, R. T. "God and Mammon." *Evangelical Quarterly* 51 (1979): 18. Quoted
in Craig L. Blomberg. *Neither Poverty nor Riches: A Biblical Theology of
Possessions.* Downers Grove, IL: InterVarsity Press, 1999.

———. *Matthew.* Tyndale New Testament Commentaries. Grand Rapids:
Eerdmans, 1985.

Fromm, Erich. *To Have or to Be?* New York: Open Road Media, 2002. Kindle
edition. Introduction.

Furnham, Adrian, and Michael Argyle. *The Psychology of Money.* New York:
Routledge, 2008. Quoted in Liezel Alsemgeest. "Talking about Money
Is Taboo: Perceptions of Financial Planning Students and Implications for the Financial Planning Industry." *Industry & Higher Education*, September 22, 2016. https://www.researchgate.net/publication
/308570708.

Gay, Craig. *Cash Values: Money and the Erosion of Meaning in Today's Society.*
Grand Rapids: Eerdmans, 2004.

———. *The Way of the (Modern) World: Or, Why It's Tempting to Live As If God
Doesn't Exist.* Grand Rapids: Eerdmans, 1998.

Georgi, G. *Remembering the Poor: The History of Paul's Collection for Jerusalem.*
Nashville: Abingdon, 1992.

Goetzmann, William. *Money Changes Everything: How Finance Made Civilization Possible.* Princeton: Princeton University Press, 2016.

Graeber, David. *Debt: The First 5,000 Years.* New York: Melville House, 2012.

Griffiths, Brian. *The Creation of Wealth: A Christian's Defense of Capitalism.*
Downers Grove, IL: InterVarsity Press, 1985.

Griffiths, Brian, and Kim Tan. *Fighting Poverty through Enterprise: The Case
for Social Venture Capital.* Coventry, UK: The Venture Centre, 2007.

Hahnel, Robert. *Of the People, by the People: The Case for a Participatory Economy.* Chico, CA: AK Press Distribution, 2012.

Haidt, Jonathan. "Three Stories about Capitalism." *Righteous Mind* (blog),
July 20, 2014. https://righteousmind.com/three-stories-about
-capitalism/.

———. "How Capitalism Changes Conscience." *Center for Humans & Nature*,
September 28, 2015. https://www.humansandnature.org/culture-how
-capitalism-changes-conscience.

Hall, D. J. *Stewardship of Life in the Kingdom of Death*. Grand Rapids: Eerd-
    mans, 1988.

Hardy, Lee. *The Fabric of This World*. Grand Rapids: Eerdmans, 1990.

Haughey, John C. *Converting Nine to Five: A Spirituality of Daily Work*. New
    York: Crossroad, 1989.

———. *The Holy Use of Money: Personal Finance in Light of Christian Faith*.
    Garden City, NY: Doubleday, 1986.

Hill, Catey. "This Number Could Predict Your Chances of Getting Divorced."
    New York Post, May 10, 2017. https://nypost.com/2017/05/10/this
    -number-could-predict-your-chances-of-getting-divorced/.

Humphrey, Caroline. "Barter and Economic Disintegration." *Man* 20: 48–72.

Ingham, Geoffrey. *The Nature of Money*. Cambridge: Polity Press, 2004.

Inglehart, Ron, and Christian Welzel. *World Values Survey*. http://www.world
    valuessurvey.org/.

Kaye, Joel. *Economy and Nature in the Fourteenth Century: Money, Market
    Exchange, and the Emergence of Scientific Thought*. Cambridge: Cam-
    bridge University Press, 1998.

Keynes, John Maynard. *Treatise on Money*. New York: Harcourt, Brace, 1930.

Kierkegaard, Søren. *Papers and Journals*. Translated by Alastair Hannay. New
    York: Penguin Books, 1996.

Krueger, David W. "A Self-Psychological View of Money." In *The Last Taboo:
    Money as Symbol and Reality in Psychotherapy and Psychoanalysis*.
    New York: Brunner/Mazel, 1986.

Kwak, Jaceeun. "Presbyterian Constitution." *Quizlet*, February 2014. http://
    quizlet.com/35814505/flasj-cards/.

Laum, Bernhard. *Heiliges Geld*. Tübingen: Mohr, 1924.

Lee, Young-hoon. *The Holy Spirit Movement in Korea: Its Historical and Theo-
    logical Development*. Oxford: Regnum Books International, 2009.

Lewis, Colin. "The Soul of Korean Christianity: How the Shamans, Buddha,
    and Confucius Paved the Way for Jesus in the Land of the Morning
    Calm." A Project for the University Scholars Program, Seattle Pacific
    University, 2014.

Luther, Martin. *Luther's Works*. American Edition. 55 vols. Edited by Jaroslav
    Pelikan. St. Louis: Concordia, 1955–86.

MacDonald, George. *The Curate's Awakening*. Minneapolis: Bethany House
    Publishers, 1985.

Mandryk, Jason. *Operation World*. Colorado Springs, CO: Biblica, 2010.

Marcovici, Philip. *The Destructive Power of Family Wealth: A Guide to Suc-*

cession Planning, Asset Protection, Taxation and Wealth Management. Hoboken, NJ: John Wiley & Sons Inc., 2016.

Marshall, I. Howard. "How Far Did the Early Christians Worship God?" *Churchman* 99, no. 3 (1985).

———. *Luke: Historian and Theologian.* Grand Rapids: Zondervan, 1974.

Marshall, Paul. *A Kind of Life Imposed on Man: Vocation and Social Order from Tyndale to Locke.* Toronto: University of Toronto Press, 1996.

Mason, Paul. *Postcapitalism: A Guide to Our Future.* Kindle ed. New York: Farrar, Straus and Giroux, 2015.

Michaelson, Robert S. "Changes in the Puritan Concept of Calling or Vocation." *New England Quarterly* 26 (1953): 315–36.

Mill, John Stuart. *Utilitarianism.* Kindle ed. Heritage Illustrated Publishing, 2014.

Mishel, Lawrence, and Jessica Schieder. "CEO Compensation Surged in 2017 Report." *Economic Policy Institute*, August 16, 2018. https://www.epi .org/publication/ceo-compensation-surged-in-2017/.

Needleman, Jacob. *Money and the Meaning of Life.* New York: Doubleday, 1991.

Newbigin, Lesslie. *Honest Religion for Secular Man.* Philadelphia: Westminster, 1966.

Nolland, John. *Luke 9:21–18:34.* Vol. 35B of *Word Biblical Commentary*, edited by David A. Hubbard, Glenn W. Barker, John D. W. Watts, and Ralph P. Martin. Dallas: Word, 1993.

Novak, Michael. *The Spirit of Democratic Capitalism.* New York: Simon & Schuster, 1982.

Oaks, Guy. "The Thing That Would Not Die: Notes on Reflection." In *Weber's Protestant Ethic: Origins, Evidence, Contexts*, edited by Hartmut Lehmann and Guenther Roth. New York: Cambridge University Press, 1993.

The Organisation for Economic Co-operation and Development (OECD). Policy Challenges for the Next 50 Years, July, 2014, 10. https://www.oecd .org/economy/Policy-challenges-for-the-next-fifty-years.pdf.

Perkins, William. *The Works of That Famous Minister of Christ in the University of Cambridge.* London: John Legatt, 1626.

Perle, Liz. *Money: A Memoir.* New York: Picador, 2006.

Poggi, Gianfranco. *Calvinism and the Capitalist Spirit: Max Weber's Protestant Ethic.* London: Macmillan, 1983.

Polanyi, Karl. *The Great Transformation: The Political and Economic Origins of Our Time.* Boston: Beacon, 2001.

Powell, Andrew. *Living Buddhism*. New York: Harmony Books, 1989.

Preece, Gordon. "Business as a Calling and Profession: Towards a Protestant Entrepreneurial Ethic." Unpublished manuscript delivered at the International Marketplace Theology Consultation, Sydney, June 2001.

Redding, Gordon. *The Spirit of Chinese Capitalism*. Berlin: de Gruyter, 1995.

Richardson, Alan. *The Biblical Doctrine of Work*. London: SCM, 1954.

Rosenberg, Nathan, and L. E. Birdzell Jr. *How the West Grew Rich: The Economic Transformation of the Industrial World*. New York: Basic Books, 1986.

Rudmin, Floyd W. "German and Canadian Data on Motivations for Ownership: Was Pythagoras Right?" Paper presented at Association for Consumer Research conference, New Orleans, LA, October 19–22, 1989.

Salkin, Jeffrey K. *Being God's Partner: How to Find the Hidden Link between Spirituality and Your Work*. Woodstock, VT: Jewish Lights Publishing, 1994.

Sandel, Michael. *What Money Can't Buy: The Moral Limits of Markets*. New York: Farrar, Straus and Giroux, 2012.

Semenova, Alla. "The Origins of Money: Evaluating Chartalist and Metallist Theories in the Context of Ancient Greece and Mesopotamia." PhD diss., University of Missouri–Kansas City, 2011. https://mospace.um system.edu/xmlui/bitstream/handle/10355/10843/SemenovaOriMon Eva.pdf.

Silverstein, Michael J., and Kate Sayre. "The Female Economy." *Harvard Business Review*, September 2009. https://hbr.org/2009/09/the-female -economy.

Simmel, Georg. *The Philosophy of Money*. Translated by Tom Bottomore and David Frisby. London: Routledge, 2004.

Sire, James W. *The Universe Next Door*. 4th ed. Downers Grove, IL: InterVarsity Press, 2004.

Smith, Adam. *The Wealth of Nations*. New York: Bantam Classic, 2003.

Smithin, John. "The Role of Money in Capitalism." *International Journal of Political Economy*, February 2002.

Sokol, Jan. "Money and the Sacred: B. Laum's Hypothesis on the Origins of Money." Lecture, Center for the Study of World Religions, Harvard University, Cambridge, MA, October 1, 2008.

Srnicek, Nick, and Alex Williams. *Inventing the Future: Postcapitalism and a World without Work*. Revised, updated ed. London: Verso Books, 2016.

Stackhouse, John, Jr. "Money in Christian History." *Vocatio* 5, no. 1 (August 2001).

Stackhouse, Max, et al. *On Moral Business: Classical and Contemporary Resources for Ethics in Economic Life.* Grand Rapids: Eerdmans, 1995.

Stevens, R. Paul. *Doing God's Business: Meaning and Motivation for the Marketplace.* Grand Rapids: Eerdmans, 2006.

———. "The Kingdom of God: Biblical Research." Institute for Marketplace Transformation. paul@imtglobal.org.

———. *The Other Six Days: Vocation, Work, and Ministry in Biblical Perspective.* Grand Rapids: Eerdmans, 2000.

———. "The Spiritual and Religious Sources of Entrepreneurship: From Max Weber to the New Business Spirituality." *Crux* 36, no. 2 (June 2000): 22-33. Reprinted in *Stimulus: The New Zealand Journal of Christian Thought and Practice* 9, no. 1 (February 2001): 2-11.

———. "Stewardship" and "Financial Support." In *The Complete Book of Everyday Christianity*, edited by Robert Banks and R. Paul Stevens, 962–67 and 419–22, respectively. Downers Grove, IL: InterVarsity Press, 1997.

———. *Work Matters: Lessons from Scripture.* Grand Rapids: Eerdmans, 2012.

Tawney, R. H. *Religion and the Rise of Capitalism.* Harmondsworth, UK: Pelican (Penguin Books), 1977.

Waltke, Bruce K. *An Old Testament Theology.* Grand Rapids: Zondervan, 2007.

Weber, Max. *The Protestant Ethic and the Spirit of Capitalism.* Mineola, NY: Dover Publications, 2003.

West, Melissa. "Tie Your Camel to the Hitching Post: An Interview with Jacob Needleman." http://www.personaltransformtion.com/jacob_needleman.html.

Woolley, Suzanne. "Your Credit Score Could Make or Break Your Love Life." *Bloomberg.com,* August 21, 2017. https://www.bloomberg.com/news/articles/2017-08-21/a-high-credit-score-can-make-you-look-sexy-on-dating.

Wright, C. J. H. *God's People in God's Land: Family, Land, and Property in the Old Testament.* Grand Rapids: Eerdmans, 1990.

Wright, N. T. *Luke for Everyone.* Louisville: Westminster John Knox, 2004.

———. *Surprised by Hope: Rethinking Heaven, the Resurrection, and the Mission of the Church.* New York: HarperOne, 2008.

———. *Matthew for Everyone*, Part 2. London: SPCK, 2002.

Zelizer, Viviana A. "Money, Power, and Sex." *Yale Journal of Law and Feminism* 18 (2006): 303. https://papers.ssrn.com/sol3/papers.cfm?abstract_id=944055.

_____. "On the Social Meaning of Money: 'Special Monies.'" *American Journal of Sociology* 95, no. 2 (September 1989): 342–77.

_____. *The Social Meaning of Money: Pin Money, Paychecks, Poor Relief, and Other Currencies*. Princeton: Princeton University Press, 2017.

Zhao Xiao. Interview by PBS. *Frontline World*. www.pbs.org/frontlineworld /stories/china_705/interview/xiao.html.

Index of Names and Subjects

National Bureau of Economic
Research, 56
National Center for the Laity, 51
Nebuchadnezzar, king of Babylonia,
35
Needleman, Jacob, xv, 1, 13–14, 42,
46, 54, 136
Newbigin, Lesslie, 134
New Covenant Baptist Church
(Washington state), 117
New Testament: kingdom worldview, xvi–xvii; message of holiness and dedicating everything
to God, 46; principle of tithing,
100, 118–19; prosperity gospel's
interpretations of verses regarding health and wealth, 118–20;
warnings about pursuit of wealth
and love of money (wealth as a
problem), xv
New Thought movement, 113–15, 117;
and generative power of positive
thought, 114; high anthropology, 114; Kenyon as founder, 117;
nineteenth-century International
New Thought Alliance, 113–14; and
priority of spiritual reality, 114; and
Swedenborg, 113. *See also* prosperity gospel movement (health and
wealth gospel)
Novak, Michael, 62

Occupy Wall Street, 38
Old Testament: the covenant and
sacred-secular dualism, 45–46;
covenant model, xv, 45–46, 98–99;
destructiveness of the pursuit
of wealth for its own sake, xv;
kingdom perspective, xvi–xvii;

and money customs in ancient
Israel, 32–33; prosperity gospel's
interpretations of, xv, 118–19; on
tithing, 100, 118, 145n3; trusteeship
and creation-mandate, 98–99;
wealth as blessing, xiv–xv
Operation World (Mandryk), 53
Organisation for Economic
Co-operation and Development
(OECD), 65
Osteen, Joel, 112–13, 121

parable of the rich fool, 125–27
parable of the rich man and the
poor man at the gate, 58, 78–79,
128
parable of the sheep and goats,
132–33
parable of the shrewd manager,
69–81, 139; and commercialized
friendship, 77–78; Jesus's message about using wealth to make
friends, 77–81; Jesus's reminder
to be both shrewd and innocent,
76–77; and kingdom of God worldview, 70–71; the manager's deals
with the master's debtors, 74–75;
as marketplace parable, 70–71;
and parable of the rich man and
the poor man Lazarus at the gate,
58, 78–79, 128; questions for reflection and discussion, 139; using
money to love ourselves and our
neighbors financially, 79–81, 101
parable of the sower, 119
participatory economies, 67
Paul the apostle: on Christ as
wealth, 134; collecting gentile
wealth for poor Jewish Christians,

Index of Scripture References